MW00426053

OH THOU WOMAN THAT BRINGEST GOOD TIDINGS

Christians for Biblical Equality
122 W Franklin Ave Ste 218
Minneapolis MN 55404-2451
Ph: 612-872-6898 Fax: 612-872-6891
Email: cbe@cbeinternational.org
Website: http://www.cbeinternational.org

OH THOU WOMAN THAT BRINGEST GOOD TIDINGS

THE LIFE AND WORK
OF KATHARINE C. BUSHNELL

Dana Hardwick

Wipf and Stock Publishers
EUGENE, OREGON

Wipf and Stock Publishers
199 West 8th Avenue, Suite 3
Eugene, Oregon 97401

Oh Thou Woman That Bringest Good Tidings
The Life and Work of Katharine C. Bushnell
By Hardwick, Dana
Copyright©1995 Hardwick, Dana
ISBN: 1-59244-067-3
Publication date: October, 2002
Previously published by Morris Publishing, 1995.

To Sharyn Dowd,
the spirit behind the words

CONTENTS

INTRODUCTION

The biblical view of the status of women in church and society has, for much of this century, been one of the most controversial issues facing Western Christianity. The authority of inspired Scripture has combined with misogynist interpretations of that Scripture to impede movement toward full equality of men and women. Consequently, advocates of equality have found it necessary to adopt an approach to Scripture that either qualifies the authority of the passages that have been used to subordinate women, or reinterprets those passages in a way that points toward equal dignity of men and women.

Although such attempts at reinterpretation are currently being done by biblical scholars in both evangelical and mainline churches and theological schools, in the late nineteenth and early twentieth centuries this was not often the case. In that period, biblical scholarship in the mainline Protestant traditions rarely focused on the reinterpretations of passages used to subordinate women; rather, such reinterpretation was done primarily by women who did not have the benefit of formal theological and exegetical training, and by a few men in the Pentecostal and Holiness traditions, which tended to appreciate the ministry of women.[1]

---

1 Lucille Sider Dayton and Donald W. Dayton, "Women in the Holiness Movement," unpublished manuscript prepared originally as a background study for a seminar led by Lucille Sider Dayton under the auspices of the Women's Aldersgate Fellowship and CHA Men at the 106th Annual Convention of the Christian Holiness Association, Louisville, Kentucky, 17–19 April 1974.

One of the most interesting efforts at reinterpreting the biblical view of women that is still in print is *God's Word to Women* by Katharine C. Bushnell. Begun in 1908 as a correspondence course for women while its author was pursuing biblical studies in England,[2] *God's Word to Women* was first published privately by Bushnell, and it continues to be reprinted and distributed by individuals interested in Bushnell's work.[3] Although the work has been publicized in the *Newsletter of the Evangelical Women's Caucus,*[4] and has influenced some popular evangelical treatments of the status of women,[5] Bushnell's interpretations seem to be largely unknown in biblical critical scholarship today.[6] Among recently published biblical commentaries, only one takes account of Bushnell's views.[7] Bushnell's treatment of the command

---

2 Ruth Hoppin, "The Legacy of Katharine Bushnell," *Update: Newsletter of the Evangelical Women's Caucus* 11 (winter 1987–88): 5–6.

3 *God's Word to Women* is available from two sources (see the annotated bibliography).

4 Ginny Hearn, "New Publishers of Katharine Bushnell," *Update: Newsletter of the Evangelical Women's Caucus* 11 (winter 1987–88): 7–8; Hoppin, "Legacy of Katharine Bushnell," 5–6.

5 Evangelicals who cite Bushnell: Jessie Penn-Lewis, *The "Magna Charta" of Woman According to the Scriptures* (Bournemouth, England: The Overcomer Book Room, 1919; reprint, Minneapolis: Bethany Fellowship, 1975); John A. Anderson, *Women's Warfare and Ministry; What Saith the Scriptures?* (Stonehaven, Great Britain: David Waldie, 1933); Joyce Harper, *Women and the Gospel* (Pinner, Great Britain: C.B.R.F. Publications, 1974); W. C. Kaiser, "Paul, Women and the Church," *Worldwide Challenge* 3 (1976): 9–12; Gilbert Bilizekian, *Beyond Sex Roles* (Grand Rapids: Baker, 1985).

6 Although it is not a critical commentary, one important recent work that cites Bushnell and offers a taste of her work from *God's Word to Women* is Letha Dawson Scanzoni and Susan Setta, "Women in Evangelical, Holiness, and Pentecostal Traditions," in vol. 3 of *Women and Religion in America: 1900–1968,* ed. Rosemary Radford Ruether and Rosemary Skinner Keller (San Francisco: Harper & Row, 1986).

7 Gordon D. Fee, *The First Epistle to the Corinthians*, New International Commentary on the New Testament (Grand Rapids: Eerdmans,

that women keep silent in the church (1 Cor. 14:34–35) is almost identical with the interpretation that is gaining acceptance among critical New Testament scholars in the present: that the command to silence is not Paul's own opinion, but a Corinthian slogan that Paul quotes in order to refute it in 14:36ff. However, most of the scholars who have argued for this interpretation seem to be unaware of Bushnell's prior work on the passage.[8] On the other hand, several scholars do cite Helen Barrett Montgomery's *Centenary Translation of the New Testament,* a work that may be dependent on Bushnell.[9]

1987). He disagrees with her. Bushnell is also cited by Linda M. Bridges, "Silencing the Corinthian Men, Not the Women," in *The New Has Come: Emerging Roles among Southern Baptist Women,* ed. Anne Thomas Neil and Virginia Garrett Neely (Washington, D.C.: Southern Baptist Alliance, 1989).

8 Some similar treatments not citing Bushnell: D. A. Carson, *Showing the Spirit: A Theological Exposition of 1 Corinthians 12–14* (Grand Rapids: Baker, 1987) (although Carson does not agree with Bushnell, he notes the treatment and cites those who do); Kaiser, "Paul, Women, and the Church" (although Kaiser cites Bushnell in this article, he does not do so with respect to her treatment of 1 Corinthians 14:33b–36); Robert W. Allison, "Let Women Be Silent in the Churches (1 Cor 14:33b–36): What Did Paul Really Say, and What Did It Mean?" *Journal for the Study of the New Testament* 32 (1988): 27–60; David W. Odell-Scott, "Let the Women Speak in Church: An Egalitarian Interpretation of 1 Cor 14:33b–36," *Biblical Theology Bulletin* 13 (1983): 90–93.

9 Sharyn Dowd, "1 Corinthians 14:34–35 as a Corinthian Slogan: The Old Roots of a 'New' Interpretation," unpublished paper read at the Southeastern Regional Meeting of the Society for Biblical Literature, 16 March 1990. Dowd finds that Helen Barrett Montgomery, *Centenary Translation of the New Testament* (Philadelphia: American Baptist Publication Society, 1924), is cited by C. H. Talbert, "Paul's Understanding of the Holy Spirit: The Evidence of 1 Corinthians 12–14," in *Perspectives on the New Testament: Essays in Honor of Frank Stagg,* ed. C. H. Talbert (Macon, GA: Mercer University Press, 1984), 95–108; Fee, *First Corinthians,* who disagrees; R. A. Bullard, "Feminine and Feminist Touches in the Centenary New Testament,"

Who was Katharine Bushnell? What kind of life engendered and nourished such out-of-step views for her time and place in history? What fostered the burning sense of centuries'-old injustice to women, so that more than once she risked her life to rectify the injustice? She was said to be fluent in seven languages, including biblical Hebrew and Greek; she was a missionary physician of considerable ability; she was well traveled; she was a central figure in at least three crusades of national and international significance for the restoration of the dignity of women. And since she did so many things so well, why is so little known about her?

Katharine Bushnell's particular mission was to bring the good tidings of freedom and equality to women everywhere, and she directed all of her talents and energies to that end. This is a study of the life and work of Katharine Bushnell, with particular attention being given to the factors that influenced her to be the "woman that bringest good tidings"[10]—to educate herself in the biblical languages, to take on the task of pointing out to women "the fallacies in the 'Scriptural' argument for the supremacy of the male sex," and to show "the true position of women in the economy of God."[11]

The Bible Translator 38 (1987): 118–22.

10 Bushnell's translation of Isaiah 40:9. Katharine C. Bushnell, *God's Word to Women: One Hundred Bible Studies on Woman's Place in the Divine Economy*, 4th ed. (Piedmont, CA: By the author, 1930), par. 209, 826.

11 Ibid., par. 1.

CHAPTER 1

BEGINNINGS

꿏

K atharine C. Bushnell was born Caroline Sophia[1] on 5 February 1855 in Peru (LaSalle County), Illinois.[2] She was the
seventh of nine children born to William Francis Bushnell and
Mary Fowler McKean Bushnell. According to her own entry in the
family Bible, Katharine had three older sisters (Sarah Elizabeth,
Mary Louisa, Lucy Rogers), three older brothers (Milton Bently,
Carlton Combs, and Edward Stone), and two younger brothers
(William Francis Jr. and John Flanagan). Frances E. Willard, a later
friend and associate, writes in a sketch of Bushnell's life[3] that her

---

1 We have been unable to discover how Bushnell's name came to be
changed to Katharine. However, her age and other information as
given in her autobiography, and the Peru, Illinois, census records
indicate that Katharine C. and Caroline Sophia are the same person.
A note in Dr. Bushnell's handwriting in the family Bible says, "This
Bible was presented to me by my mother, Mary Fowler Bushnell, at
our home in Evanston, Ill. in October 1893." It is signed "Katharine
C. Bushnell (baptised Caroline Sophia)."

2 This date of birth is given in family records that were copied and
sent to me by Bushnell's great-niece, Peg Moor, presently residing
in San Bruno, California. The date is borne out by the 1860 census
form, which lists Bushnell's age as five years on 1 June 1860. In her
autobiography, Bushnell gives her age as twenty-four in October
1879. It is interesting that secondary sources give her year of birth
as 1856: Frances E. Willard, ed., *A Woman of the Century* (Buffalo,
NY: Moolton, 1893), 141; Hoppin, "Legacy of Katharine Bushnell."

3 Willard makes the only reference we have to Horace Bushnell, David
Bushnell, and John Rogers as ancestors of Katharine Bushnell.

13

family was an interesting and illustrious one whose ancestors included John Rogers, the Smithfield martyr;[4] Horace Bushnell, a pioneering liberal theologian, author, and clergyman in Hartford, Connecticut, said to be "one of the most creative and liberal minds in 19th century American theology";[5] and David Bushnell, the inventor of the first American submarine, used unsuccessfully in the Revolutionary War.[6] Bushnell's father was a carpenter[7] who worked for the government as a building contractor.[8] Little is known about Katharine's early years, except that she attended the public schools, was a member of the Methodist Episcopal Church, and was converted when she was seventeen years old.[9]

Education

In 1873, at the age of eighteen, Bushnell entered the preparatory school of Northwestern University to take a literary course.[10] Shortly thereafter she entered the university, where she

---

Frances E. Willard, "Dr. Kate Bushnell, A Sketch," *The Union Signal* 16 (20 November 1890), 4 (National Headquarters, WCTU [Joint Ohio Historical Society—Michigan Historical Collections—WCTU microfilm edition]), roll 6, frame 512 (hereafter cited as WCTU microfilm edition).

4   Willard, *Woman of the Century.*

5   William D. Halsey, ed., *Collier's Encyclopedia* (New York: Macmillan Educational Company, 1985), s.v. "Horace Bushnell" by Barbara M. Cross.

6   Bernard S. Cayne, ed., *Encyclopedia Americana,* international ed. (Danbury, CT: Grolier, 1986), "David Bushnell" by Joyce L. Myers. According to Myers, David disappeared after the war and reappeared in Georgia under an assumed name.

7   Photocopy of page from census of 1860 in which her family appears. Bushnell's father, William Bushnell, has his occupation listed as "carpenter." Photocopy received from Peru Public Library, Peru, Illinois.

8   Willard, "Bushnell, A Sketch."

9   Ibid.

10 Katharine C. Bushnell, *Dr. Katharine C. Bushnell: A Brief Sketch of Her Life Work* (Hertford, England: Rose & Sons, 1932), 3; Willard, "Bushnell, A Sketch."

studied classics for two years. While living in Evanston and attending college, Bushnell also studied medicine as a private student of Dr. James S. Jewell, who was noted in both Europe and the United States for his work in nerve diseases. She was a friend of the Jewell family and spent much time in their home.[11]

At Northwestern Bushnell became a student of Frances Willard, dean of the Women's College, who was to be a great influence on the course of Bushnell's life. Willard had been president of the Evanston College for Ladies, a Methodist women's college that was assimilated into Northwestern University, admission to which had previously been restricted to male students. After "acrimonious disputes" with Northwestern's president, to whom she had briefly been engaged many years before, Willard resigned her position as dean in 1874 and became heavily involved in temperance reform work, later becoming president of the Women's Christian Temperance Union (WCTU).[12]

After two years, Bushnell found that her focus had changed and, for undisclosed reasons,[13] she left the college and entered The Woman's Hospital Medical College.[14] Bushnell's nephew gives a brief description of this part of her medical training, relating that "professors put a screen around her in classes so she could get up and recite without being seen, at which the 'men'

---

11 Willard, *Woman of the Century,* 141; Hoppin, "Legacy of Katharine Bushnell"; Willard, "Bushnell, A Sketch."

12 Zadel Barnes Gustafson, "Frances E. Willard," *The Christian* 981 (2 December 1887), photocopy.

13 Bushnell, *Brief Sketch,* 3. It is possible that this decision had something to do with Willard's precipitate departure from Northwestern the year before, since Willard and Bushnell had developed a close relationship and Willard referred to Bushnell as being a strong and "chivalric ally" at this time (Willard, "Bushnell, A Sketch"). Bushnell had also known Willard as a close neighbor of her parents in Evanston (Bushnell, *Brief Sketch,* 5).

14 The Woman's Hospital Medical College was later purchased by Northwestern, and eventually merged with Rush Medical College when the latter began to admit women as students. Bushnell, *Brief Sketch,* 3.

in the room would hoot and yell."[15] She was graduated four years later, in 1879, younger by three years than her fellow students.[16]

Missionary Work in China

After graduation at age twenty-four and a brief internship,[17] Bushnell served as a resident physician in the Hospital for Women and Children in Chicago.[18] Although she wished to continue her medical education with more clinical and postgraduate work, she was soon persuaded by the Women's Mission Board of the Methodist Episcopal Church to go to Kiukiang, China, as a missionary. The work was exhausting and stressful, for personnel were scarce and facilities were primitive. Bushnell frequently found herself performing surgery, acting as her own anesthetist, and doing all the nursing besides. She was not happy in Kiukiang, which is near Shanghai, relating that "this was the mistake of my life, excepting that 'All things work together for good to them that love God.'" She felt that she was "too young for the heavy strain that fell to [her] lot,"[19] and she remained intensely homesick.[20]

---

15 William Bushnell Stout, *So Away I Went* (New York: Bobbs-Merrill, 1951), 53. The account given here also includes the information that Bushnell was the "first woman graduate of Northwestern Medical School," which is not true. Stout's niece (Bushnell's great-niece) relates in a personal note that Stout "was a great story teller and I cannot vouch for the accuracy of the material he wrote about Dr. Bushnell."

16 Bushnell, *Brief Sketch*, 3.

17 *Women's Medical School: Northwestern University (Woman's Medical College of Chicago) Class Histories 1870–1890* (Chicago: H. G. Butler, Publisher, 1896), 137, photocopy.

18 Willard, *Woman of the Century*, 141; Willard, "Bushnell, A Sketch." Neither article mentions the locale of the Hospital for Women and Children. Since Willard mentions the residency immediately after talking about Bushnell's education at the Woman's Medical College in Chicago, we are assuming that this was in Chicago also.

19 Bushnell, *Brief Sketch*, 3–4.

20 "Our Third and Fourth Round-the-World Missionaries in the Orient," *The Union Signal* 20 (23 August 1894), 4 (WCTU microfilm edition), roll 9, frame 569.

Despite the hardships and her homesickness, Bushnell had a thriving practice in Kiukiang, her popularity having been enhanced by her successful treatment of a gateman who had been attacked by robbers and left for dead. According to Bushnell, the "rumour went abroad throughout the city and surrounding country, that the gateman died seven times during that night, and I had medicine that brought him to life again." Bushnell became so popular that the missionaries feared a mob uprising if she were called upon again to raise the dead. Knowing she could not live up to her reputation, she was forced to retreat into the mountains until the rumors died down.[21]

Bushnell's poor health demanded that she spend a good deal of time in the mountains, where the missionaries had built a small hut as a retreat from exposure to the heat and pestilence in the city. She sometimes "sat week after week able to do little but watch the play of the sunlight on these mountains." A former classmate, Dr. Ella Gilchrist, was sent to join her in her missionary medical practice. Gilchrist's presence gave her some much-needed relief, and her health improved somewhat.[22] During her third summmmer in Kiukiang, however, while she was resting in the mountains, Bushnell seriously injured her spine, thus cutting short her missionary career in China.[23] About this time, Gilchrist became seriously ill with tuberculosis, and the two doctors returned home. Bushnell left China feeling that her whole life had been a failure.[24] However, she retained many good memories also,

---

21 Bushnell, *Brief Sketch*, 5, 3–4.

22 "Round-the-World Missionaries in the Orient."

23 Bushnell, *Brief Sketch*, 5. Bushnell says this injury was to bother her somewhat for the rest of her life. However, she never again mentions it in the writings we have been able to examine. In a *Union Signal* article (20 November 1890) on Bushnell, Willard says she returned home because Gilchrist was mortally ill, but Bushnell says it was because of her own failing health (*Brief Sketch*, 4, 5; "Round-the-World Missionaries in the Orient").

24 *Class Histories*, 137; "Round-the-World Missionaries in the Orient." Ella M. Gilchrist was a graduate of the same medical school (class of 1881). She died of tuberculosis shortly after her return home, with Bushnell at her bedside.

and when she returned twelve years later in a different capacity she enjoyed her reunion with both places and people she had known then. Although Bushnell does not say much about the positive impact of her work in China, secondary sources claim that she established a pediatric hospital in Kiukiang.[25]

It was in China, however, that Bushnell first began to observe the effects a male-dominated society had on its women, and the lengths to which this domination could drive those women. She relates an incident occurring during her time there in which a mother, whose daughter's bound feet had grown too large for the shoes she had made, attempted to cut the daughter's feet to the size of the shoes with her scissors.[26]

It was also in China that Bushnell began to feel the call to deeper and more critical Bible study. She states that at the time of her going to China, she believed "it was neither desirable nor necessary for women to preach the Gospel; it was unbecoming."[27] During her travels in China, however, she encountered a sex-biased translation of a passage in the Chinese translation of the Bible, and when she questioned a male missionary,

> he said that undoubtedly it was so rendered because of pagan prejudice against the ministry of women. I was shocked. It has never before entered my mind that such a thing could be. This led to my tracing other signs, both in the Chinese and the English Bible, that pointed in the same direction, when I consulted my Greek Testament.[28]

As she began to study both the Chinese and the English Bibles, her opinions as to the place of women in the gospel began

---

25 Hoppin, "Legacy of Katharine Bushnell"; Stout, *Away I Went,* 53. Hoppin says the hospital was at Shanghai, Stout at Kiukiang. As Kiukiang is quite near Shanghai, and as Bushnell was a medical missionary in Kiukiang, it is probable that this is the same hospital.
26 Bushnell, *God's Word to Women,* par. 656.
27 Bushnell, *Brief Sketch,* 20.
28 Ibid. Bushnell presumably began her study of Greek during her classics course at Northwestern.

to change. "Could it be possible that men allowed prejudice to colour Scripture translation?"[29]

Medical Practice and Early Work with WCTU

Returning to the United States with the ailing Ella Gilchrist in 1882, Bushnell accompanied Gilchrist to her home in Denver, Colorado, where Bushnell remained with her until her death.[30] Bushnell established a medical practice in Denver but was discontented with the work.[31] It was during her time in Denver that she first became associated with the Women's Christian Temperance Union, more specifically with the Department for Advancement of Social Purity.[32] She took charge of the Chinese Departments of the West, due to her experience in China and the "devoted attachment of the Chinese" to her.[33] She also superintended work among "fallen women" (prostitutes) for the WCTU in Denver[34] and was active in establishing, christening, and contributing to the Denver WCTU's chapter newspaper, *The Challenge.*[35] In 1884, Bushnell also was active in a Denver club that studied heredity, offering biweekly lectures at the club from

---

29   Ibid.

30   "A Good Work," *The Inter Ocean,* Chicago, 13 February 1886, photocopy from Willard Scrapbook. All scrapbook copies from National Headquarters, WCTU (Joint Ohio Historical Society—Michigan Historical Collections—WCTU microfilm edition) unless otherwise noted.

31   Bushnell, *Brief Sketch,* 5; K. Fillmore Gray, "Crusader: California Woman's career reads like a movie scenario," *The Christian Advocate,* 8 January 1942, photocopy received from Peg Moor.

32   *Class Histories,* 137.

33   Minutes of National Women's Christian Temperance Union Convention (1884), xliv, xlv, photocopy received from Frances Willard Memorial Library for Alcohol Research, National Women's Christian Temperance Union, Evanston, Illinois.

34   *The Union Signal* 12 (4 March 1886), photocopy received from Hoppin.

35   Editorial in *The Challenge,* 2 September 1886, photocopy received from Frances Willard Memorial Library.

November to May, and sending circular letters to Union chapters.[36]

In 1885, Willard persuaded Bushnell to come to Chicago as National Evangelist of the social purity department of the WCTU. Of the "social purity" work, Willard said,

> Some sporadic efforts had been made in this direction [i.e., speaking in opposition to abuses against prostitutes] from time to time, but the action of our Philadelphia Convention in 1885 launched the new lifeboat nationally, and because no other woman could be found to stand at its helm I have tried to do so, though utterly unable to give this great work an attention more than fragmentary.[37]

So Bushnell gave up her medical practice in Denver and moved to Illinois in February of 1886.[38] She was not unhappy about changing professions, for she "had not studied medicine for its own sake, but as a help in Christian work,"[39] and she felt that God was now calling her to a more important work. Bushnell brought with her from Denver a "reformed fallen woman" who was to help her greatly with her work in Chicago. Before Ella Gilchrist's death, she and Bushnell had rescued Bertha Lyons from her life in the streets, taking her into their home and reforming her from her former ways. Lyons was "converted" beside Gilchrist's deathbed.[40]

In Chicago, Bushnell and Lyons became active in the establishment and supervision of reading rooms, where meetings were held with the women two or more times a day. During the day Bushnell would canvass the neighborhoods in which the reading rooms were located, "inviting women to come to the meeting, where, after singing and prayer, she [would] talk to them urging them to forsake a life of sin, and by personal effort help all who

---

36 Minutes of the National WCTU Convention, xcvii.
37 Frances E. Willard, *Glimpses of Fifty Years: The Autobiography of an American Woman* (Chicago: H. J. Smith & Co., 1889), 419.
38 Bushnell, *Brief Sketch*, 5–6; Willard, *Woman of the Century*, 141; Minutes of National WCTU Convention, xxxvi; *Class Histories*, 131.
39 Bushnell, *Brief Sketch*, 5.
40 *The Challenge*, 4 March 1886, photocopy; "Good Work."

wish to reform to do so and obtain employment."[41] She "did rescue work for the city missions"[42] and was also responsible for the founding of the Anchorage Mission in Chicago, a rescue mission for women and girls that sheltered and cared for up to five thousand women a year.[43]

The Anchorage Mission had been Willard's dream, but it was brought to fruition through the efforts of Bushnell and Elizabeth Wheeler Andrew,[44] a co-worker in the social purity department of the WCTU. Bushnell and Andrew began the Anchorage Mission as a simple reading room that would shelter women and girls during the day and provide them with a light meal. At night, however, the women would have to go back out on the streets, or to their old places of business. The reading room was very successful, and it quickly became apparent that a more permanent shelter was needed for those who wished to leave the life of prostitution. Within a short time, through the contributions of concerned women, the WCTU was able to purchase a house in the heart of the red-light district, "surrounded on all sides by vile dens, saloons and dance houses." The women could live in the mission free of charge until they returned home or found decent work. Willard called the mission "a clearing house of sinners, and . . . to some extent at least, of sin."[45]

Bushnell and her corps of women volunteers actively sought out those women who were caught in the seemingly inescapable net of prostitution and vice. These volunteers read the morning newspapers and police records to get the names and whereabouts of the latest offenders and went searching for them, offering them a faith and a future. They handed small printed

---

41 *The Union Signal* 12 (22 April 1886), photocopy.

42 Stout, *So Away I Went,* 53.

43 Willard, *Woman of the Century,* 141; *Class Histories,* 134; Hoppin, "Legacy of Katharine Bushnell," 5.

44 Bushnell, *Brief Sketch,* 3. Andrew would spend the next twenty-five years as Bushnell's "companion in labor." Andrew was also associate editor of *The Union Signal* until she and Bushnell took up their duties as world evangelists for the newly formed World WCTU.

45 Frances Willard, "Our White-Ribbon Anchorage," *The Union Signal* 18 (20 October 1892), 9 (WCTU microfilm edition), roll 8, frame 282.

invitations to their meetings to women entering saloons or walking the streets.

Bushnell was not naive about the work she was doing. She advised her workers "against trusting implicitly girls who come professing a desire to reform . . . and against making large promises, or failing to more than fulfill those made." She advised the women who reformed to keep their pasts to themselves "so long as it could be truthfully done, but never to sacrifice truth to expediency." She felt that "their liberty in regard to marriage with pure men should be the same as that accorded reformed men in regard to marriage with pure women."[46]

Bushnell's long-range plan was for the establishment of various reading rooms and inexpensive lodging houses in the less desirable neighborhoods of large towns and cities, and for notices of their availability to be posted in train depots and public places. Bushnell distributed circulars encouraging concerned women to visit "degraded women" (prostitutes), to pray with them, to convert them from their line of work, and, as in the case with the Anchorage Mission, to find suitable employment for them or to send them back to their homes.[47]

Bushnell crossed and recrossed the country, lecturing and preaching about social purity and giving instructions to local WCTU chapters about setting up reading rooms similar to those in Chicago. She was on the road for months at a time, traveling by train and living as a guest in the homes of local WCTU members. She was paid no salary, but lived on the donations and hospitality of those to whom she lectured. Her travel time was spent in Bible study, in the study of biblical languages,[48] and in writing articles for *The Union Signal* and pamphlets for the social purity department.

The area in which Katharine Bushnell was employed, as National Evangelist for the Department of Social Purity of the WCTU, did not constitute the primary work of the organization, but was a natural consequence of it. The primary aim of the

---

46 "Points from Lake Bluff Training School," *The Union Signal* 12 (26 August 1886), 2 (WCTU microfilm edition), roll 3, frame 376.
47 Ibid.
48 Bushnell, *Brief Sketch*, 20.

WCTU was that of universal temperance,[49] and, while Willard, the founder and president of the WCTU, showed herself deeply concerned with the issues of social purity, her attention to the Department of Social Purity was admittedly fragmentary and her principal focus was temperance.[50]

Bushnell, however, showed little interest in the issue of temperance except as it was related to social purity, although she did equate the presence and the high-cost licensing of liquor with the development of "trade in shame." In a speech in Vermont during the spring of 1889 she said that "the man who votes the low groggery out and high license in, votes in the den of infamy also."[51] The abuses resulting from drink, which admittedly were many, she felt were symptoms of a deeper problem. Her writing reflects that she found the cause of the degradation of women not in the abuses resulting from drink, but in the bias of both the writing and the translations of the Bible by males.[52] From the time in China when she first realized that bias in translation could be deliberate, she directed her energies not only to the reformation and healing of the women and the society who were victims of that bias, but also to the education of all women, including herself, in the Bible and the biblical languages so that the questionable passages could be reinterpreted.

Around this time, Bushnell began to read about allegations of "white slavery" in the lumber camps of northern Wisconsin and Michigan, where the influx of large numbers of laborers for iron mining and felling of trees encouraged "the criminal industry of enticing young girls to go north under promises of lucrative work."[53] When nobody could be found to investigate the conditions and get reliable facts, Bushnell determined to investigate them for herself. Thus began the first of Dr. Katharine Bushnell's great crusades.

---

49   Ibid., 8.
50   Willard, *Glimpses of Fifty Years,* 419.
51   *The Union Signal* 15 (14 March 1889), 12 (WCTU microfilm edition), roll 5, frame 420.
52   Bushnell, *God's Word to Women,* lessons 77–79, par. 616–44; Bushnell, *Brief Sketch,* 20.
53   Ibid., 6.

CHAPTER 2

WISCONSIN
LUMBER CAMPS

🙰

A fter becoming extremely "exercised" by the increasing
  number of reports in the daily press of the existence of a
white slave trade, Bushnell and officials of the local WCTU chapters in Michigan and Wisconsin began working to get state officials to check into the reports. These reports suggested that
atrocities were being committed against women and girls; that
mentally retarded women were being taken and held; even that
some of the stockades in which the women were being held were
guarded by dogs.[1] As state officials proved reluctant to investigate the conditions and get the facts,[2] Bushnell spent May, June,
July, and August of 1888 in northern Wisconsin for this purpose.[3]

A state investigator, James Fielding, who had been sent to
inquire into these abuses, reported his findings as negative,
requiring "no necessity for state interference in the matter."[4]
Bushnell, however, had conversations with Fielding, the "gover-

---

1 Katharine Bushnell, "Work in Northern Wisconsin: Dr. Bushnell's
   Investigation," *W.C.T.U. State Work* (Madison, Wisconsin), 3 (November 1888): 1–7, photocopy. There is some ambiguity as to
   whether Bushnell presented the report at the national WCTU convention in New York City, 18 October 1888, or whether someone
   read her report.
2 Bushnell, *Brief Sketch*, 6.
3 *The Union Signal* 15 (10 January 1889), 1 (WCTU microfilm edition),
   roll 5, frame 314.
4 Ibid.

nor's detective," who admitted that he had never done the investigations about which he had written.[5] He had been to only one town, had entered only one den, and had interviewed only the one group of inmates found in that den.[6] Fielding admitted to Bushnell that the dens did exist, that women were "detained" for payment of fines levied by the house for misbehaviors of various kinds, and that their clothes and wages were withheld pending payment of such fines. Fielding had written a completely ficitious report that was published in the *Milwaukee Journal,* saying that he found no evidence of abduction, enticement, or involuntary detention of women or girls from Milwaukee and Chicago in the many brothels he claimed to have inspected.[7]

Bushnell was not, of course, satisfied with the state of affairs as reported by Fielding, and she began her investigation. She had planned to spend only one month on her inquiries, but that month stretched to four. It was at considerable risk that Bushnell entered the brothels and stockades in which the women were being held. She compiled information both from those who aided women in escape attempts and from her own observations. She interviewed ministers, doctors, lawyers, and escapees from the "infamous dens."[8] In one place she entered, she was able to interview the cook to get a view of the life led by the women working in the house.[9] Using methods she learned while working with prostitutes in the larger cities, step by step she compiled her report.[10]

Bushnell's method was to take a story or a rumor and attempt to ascertain the provable facts. This approach, of course,

---

5 Bushnell, "Work in Northern Wisconsin," 1.

6 *The Union Signal* 15 (10 January 1889), 1 (WCTU microfilm edition), roll 5, frame 314.

7 "Where Satan Rules," *Milwaukee Journal,* 7 February 1887, as reprinted in Bushnell's report to the WCTU National Convention, 18 October 1888.

8 *The Union Signal* 15 (10 January 1889), 1 (WCTU microfilm edition), roll 5, frame 314.

9 Kate C. Bushnell, "The Facts in the Case," *The Union Signal* 15 (7 March 1889), 5 (WCTU mocrofilm edition) roll 5, frame 382.

10 Bushnell, "Work in Northern Wisconsin," 2.

led down many blind alleys. She would search for reliable witnesses having personal knowledge of and involvement in the case under investigation. She insisted on talking to inmates, viewing the situation for herself. One side of a story, from one witness only, was not enough. In cases where she did use the testimony of only one "degraded woman" or one "degraded man," she explained in her report why she accepted the testimony.[11] Having penetrated the brothels by one excuse or another, she was able by various pretexts to obtain proof of the conditions that existed there. The previous reports she had heard of women and girls being detained and guarded by dogs she found to be true. She was able to make sketches from within one of the stockaded and guarded dens, and made several outside sketches of the more notorious places.[12]

Bushnell was not without aid in her investigations. She found more than willing help from members of the local chapters of the WCTU and ministers in the towns and villages in which she was making her inquiries. When she was in danger, there were always Christian friends or sympathetic ministers within calling distance, and she was careful to keep someone aware at all times of where she was going. In the four months of her study, she investigated nearly sixty dens and compiled information on 577 "degraded women," many of whom she interiewed personally.[13]

Bushnell found cases of young girls, a few of whom were only thirteen or fourteen years old, being forced to live as prostitutes. She found women who were kept in subjection by whip, fist, boot, and bulldog. A woman in Ashland, Wisconsin, was murdered by being soaked in oil and then set aflame. The man who did this was named in the verdict of the coroner's jury, which read "burned to death by W. H. Griffin." Griffin was never charged or prosecuted. In some places police responded to pleas for help by women trying to get free, but in far too many others, the police refused assistance, sometimes even returning runaways to their brothels. Bushnell found cases of the use of blatantly purchased

---

11 Ibid.
12 Bushnell, *Brief Sketch*, 6.
13 *The Union Signal* 14 (8 November 1888), 4 (WCTU microfilm edition), roll 5, frame 234.

political influence to stop legal action from being taken. False reports were filed by politicians who owed their position and influence to men who had grown rich on the proceeds from the "dance halls" and "dens."[14]

In her conversations with the medical personnel who had dealings with the prostitutes, Bushnell found that in effect the women were being licensed to practice prostitution. Many of the towns housing brothels had strict "Contagious Diseases Acts," modeled on those in England, requiring frequent examination of women working in houses "where such diseases exist, or are likely to be contracted." In some towns these examinations were conducted at public expense. Bushnell found that the doctors largely supported the existence of the houses of prostitution because of the extra income they derived from examining the women. The hospital and health officials of one town favored opening a brothel "for the sake of the practice it would afford them." One of them estimated that fully 60 percent of his patients were to come as the result of the opening of the den. Bushnell had in her possession copies of the certificates kept by the physicians for the purpose of certifying the health of the women so "that they can assure their male associates that they may sin, with all immunity from physical danger."[15] In one town the physician who signed the certificate was the mayor.

Another thing Bushnell discovered during her research was that some townspeople were by no means eager to see this industry removed from among them. In one town, the "den-keeper" had been closed down by citizens and the den burned. During the summer of the following year, the businessmen met and decided it would be better for their own businesses if the keeper were allowed to return and resume operations. The bordello was rebuilt, the re-opening heralded in the local newspaper, and invitations sent to each of the businessmen.[16]

It was not that there were no laws prohibiting the operation of such houses of ill repute. On 9 March 1887, largely due to the efforts of the Wisconsin chapter of the WCTU's social purity

---

14 Bushnell, "Work in Northern Wisconsin," 5, 3.
15 Ibid., 3–4.
16 Ibid.

section, Senate Bill 46, headed "An Act for the prevention of crime and to prevent the abducting of unmarried women," was passed by the Wisconsin Senate. This bill made it illegal to abduct unmarried women "of previous chaste character," to detain women by force in houses of "ill fame," to use a mentally ill woman for purposes of prostitution, or to allow women under the age of twenty-one to be taken or used for immoral purposes.[17] There was also a law against "trading in vice," but since this behavior was punished by fines instead of imprisonment, the effect of the law was to license the brothels rather than to shut them down.[18] Economic considerations kept the laws from being enforced, and the "previous chaste character" clause of the law protecting women from abduction and imprisonment for immoral purposes allowed the houses to be staffed. Procurers were "allowed to defend themselves against a charge of present fraud by proving a past sin in the victim."[19]

In spite of all the horror Bushnell witnessed, and the frequent cases in which women were held against their wills by stockades, vicious dogs, and other means, she found that the real obstacles to their return to a "virtuous life" to be, first,

> a total lack of sympathy for the girl in her terrible fate, on the part of men, women and officers of the law. [Second,] a persistent determination to maintain these houses as a 'necessity' and regulate the evil by compelling all girls whose appearances are against them, to live in the houses. [Third,] a demand on the part of *virtuous* (God forgive the misnomer!) women that their virtue be protected by the degradation of young girls.[20]

Bushnell reported these finding at a WCTU meeting in Chicago, and she became an overnight sensation as newspapers

---

17 *Laws of Wisconsin,* Chapter 214, Laws of 1887, no. 46, S. Published 28 April 1887, introduced by Senator Ware and passed 9 March 1887. Photocopy received from The State of Wisconsin Legislative Reference Bureau, Madison, Wisconsin.

18 *W.C.T.U. State Work* 2 (December 1887), 1, photocopy.

19 Bushnell, "Work in Northern Wisconsin," 4.

20 Ibid., 7.

rushed to get in on the latest furor. Exaggerated reports of her investigations appeared eveywhere. Even *The Union Signal*, organ of the national WCTU, published information that was unsubstantiated and exaggerated, but it later printed her article repudiating the inaccuracies. Bushnell accused the newspapers of deliberately distorting the facts as she had presented them. "I believe this has been wilfully and maliciously done in order to arouse indignation against me, and to throw discredit upon my own truthful statements."[21]

Bushnell was not the only one to suffer. Those who had supported her came in for their share of abuse. A Methodist paster in Wausau, Wisconsin, the Reverend John Scott Davis, had stood surety for Dr. Bushnell's word, and as a result was arrested for libel and tried, although he was acquitted.[22]

Bushnell herself was accosted and verbally abused by Fielding, the governor's investigator, who "broke in angrily upon a conversation, without any reasonable provokation [sic], to insult Miss Bushnell by calling her a liar and telling a story he heard from the lips of Mike Leahy, the dive keeper, charging her with unchastity." Bushnell proferred charges against him, and Fielding did not deny the charges. After five continuances on the part of Fielding, a mixup in dates caused prosecuting attorney Olin to request a continuance, at which point Madison Municipal Judge E. W. Keys refused Olin's request and "promptly dismissed the case, elaborating on the fact that Fielding was 'completely exonerated of the charge against him.'"[23]

Wisconsin officials denied Bushnell's reports and heaped abuse on her for slandering their state.[24] When she appeared before an out-of-session meeting of the Wisconsin legislature, she had to be protected by police from possible violence. Initially overwhelmed by her position as the only woman in a room full of hostile men, and being a woman of prayer, she "lifted her heart

---

21 Bushnell, "Facts in the Case."
22 Mary E. McDowell, "A Noble Defender," *The Union Signal* 15 (4 November 1889), 5 (WCTU microfilm edition), roll 5, frame 425.
23 "Truth about the Fielding Case," *W.C.T.U. State Work* 4 (June 1889), 5, photocopy.
24 Bushnell, *Brief Sketch*, 7.

to God," whereupon "the door opened quietly, and about fifty ladies of the highest social position at the State Capital filed in, and stood all about me. There were no seats for them; they stood all the time I talked—and I had plenty of courage as I realized how good God was to send them!"[25]

There was other support for Bushnell. Copies of her report were printed and distributed by the Wisconsin WCTU. Resolutions were adopted all over the country praising Bushnell for her work, condemning those who condoned prostitution, and requesting legislatures to enact laws that would severely punish and suppress such activity.[26] Towns and ministerial associations in Wisconsin, Maine, Illinois, Pennsylvania, Indiana, and many other states adopted resolutions and pledged to support and further the work begun by Bushnell and the Wisconsin WCTU.[27] The result of her work was the passage of a bill nicknamed "The Kate Bushnell Bill," which dealt with the issues she had been investigating. While Bushnell said that she had no part in its drafting, the newspapers gave her the credit and the bill her name.[28]

---

25 *Oakland Tribune,* 10 February 1946, obituary; Bushnell, *Brief Sketch,* 7.

26 The laws currently in force levied fines. The resolutions requested that these laws would exact imprisonment rather than fines for violations, as the fines were considered licensing fees by violaters. When such a bill had been passed by the legislature (replacing fines with five to ten years of imprisonment), the governor failed to sign it into law (*W.C.T.U. State Work* 2 [December 1887], 1).

27 "Sustain Dr. Kate Bushnell," *W.C.T.U. State Work* 4 (March 1889), 4; *The Union Signal* 15 (11 April 1889), 5; (21 February 1889), 8; (6 June 1889), 11; 31 January 1889; etc. (all from WCTU microfilm edition), roll 5.

28 Bushnell, *Brief Sketch,* 7. There is some confusion about exactly what bill this is. Inquiries to The State Historical Society of Wisconsin and The State of Wisconsin Legislative Reference Bureau elicited no information on any bill other than Senate Bill 46, which was passed 9 March 1887, more than a year before Bushnell had been fighting for a change from fines to prison sentences for those operating houses of prostitution and the removal of the "previous

In her autobiography, Frances Willard lauded Bushnell's effort, writing that "the heroic doctor is going everywhere and has made such a reconnoissance of the North Woods lumber camps as ought to place her name among the Grace Darlings of moral rescue work."[29] Bushnell found her new reputation to be a hindrance to her work of evangelism, however. Her popularity increased so greatly after the report on Wisconsin that *The Union Signal* was forced to print a notice reminding those interested in obtaining Bushnell's services as a speaker that she could speak only once a day.[30] But wherever she went to speak, the audience preferred the "sensational stories about Northern Wisconsin" to the "plain moral instruction in the principles of purity, such as had been previously well received."[31]

That year the national convention of the WCTU was held in New York City, but Bushnell was not on the program, in spite of the magnitude of her contribution and the fact that "the whole country was agitated on the white slave question by the disclosures" her investigations had brought to light. However, Bushnell herself admitted that the major focus of the WCTU was temperance and realized "its interests must not be diverted."[32] The sooner the sensationalism faded, the better, as her primary message of social purity was not being heard because of it.[33]

Bushnell went home to Evanston to think and to pray for God's guidance for light on the future direction of her ministry. She saw little use in continuing to speak on the social purity question until the sensation of the lumber camps faded, but she feared that the furor may have branded her message perma-

---

chaste character" clause, and since she later talks about prison sentences issued to offenders, it may well have been that the "Kate Bushnell Bill" dealt with some like aspect.

29 Willard, *Glimpses of Fifty Years, 419.*
30 *The Union Signal* 15 (11 April 1889), 1 (WCTU microfilm edition), roll 5, frame 423.
31 Bushnell, *Brief Sketch,* 8.
32 Ibid.
33 The fact that Bushnell mentions not being on the program suggests that her "realization" is not entirely sincere. (See n. 1.)

nently. "I did not wish to keep an unhealthy sensation alive; legislation having been secured, I wished the matter dropped."[34]

One warm summer afternoon in 1890, Bushnell was seeking guidance from the Bible, and twice in a row her selection fell on references in both the Old and New Testaments to Joseph's dreams. The third turning of pages resulted in the story of Peter's dream on Simon the tanner's rooftop in the city of Joppa. After saying to herself, "Why could I not be guided by a dream?" [35] she fell asleep. She records that she dreamed that she had been tossed about on the waves on a voyage to England to see Josephine Butler, the head of the Social Purity Department in England's WCTU, and to do some work for her.[36] After initial hesitation, she decided that God had provided the guidance for which she had been praying. She promptly wrote Butler, telling her of the dream, and since Butler "saw no reason to doubt that the vision vouchsafed to Kate Bushnell was of God,"[37] Butler wrote and invited Bushnell to come to England because she might have work for her in an Indian campaign for purity.

This invitation fell in with Bushnell's plans in other ways, also. She had been chosen by the officers of the newly formed World WCTU as world evangelist. She and Elizabeth Andrew, her co-evangelist, were to travel around the world, speaking in the interests of social purity.[38] Willard encouraged Bushnell to take this trip, feeling that "it would be better for [her] to pursue [her] purity activities where it could be done with less sensation because of the Wisconsin episode."[39] However, Bushnell was definitely still willing to speak on the subject of forced prostitution in Wisconsin and to put the facts, however disagreeable,

---

34 Bushnell, *Brief Sketch*, 8.

35 Ibid.

36 Ibid., 8–9; Glen Petrie, *A Singular Iniquity: The Campaigns of Josephine Butler* (New York: Viking, 1971), 266; Enid Hester Chataway Moberly Bell, *Josephine Butler: Flame of Fire* (London: Constable and Co., Ltd., 1962), 229.

37 Petrie, *Singular Iniquity*, 267.

38 *The Union Signal* 16 (25 December 1890), 16 (WCTU microfilm edition), roll 6, frame 563; Willard, "Bushnell, A Sketch."

39 Bushnell, *Brief Sketch*, 9.

before her listeners. She gained funding for her trip (for which there was to be provided neither salary nor expenses) by public speaking.[40] Speaking in Berea, Ohio, in December of 1890, only one month before she sailed for England, Bushnell told her audience, "I know these facts are not pleasant to hear . . . but you *shall* hear them."[41] Then Katharine Bushnell prepared to set sail for England.

---

40 Ibid., 10.

41 *The Union Signal* 16 (25 December 1890), 11 (WCTU microfilm edition), roll 9, frame 560.

CHAPTER 3

CRUSADE
IN INDIA

D uring the mid-Victorian era, Josephine Butler (1828–1906) was the outstanding figure promoting moral reform in England. Her main interest was in "the reclamation of prostitutes and the suppression of the 'white slave' trade. . . . Behind her activities as a reformer lay a life of almost continuous prayer."[1] She started her work in Liverpool in 1866 and continued to work among prostitutes for forty years—the rest of her life—despite continuous opposition, conflict, and misunderstanding.[2] Her husband of thirty-eight years, a Canon of Winchester Cathedral, was her partner and her support throughout her crusades.

There were many parallels between Katharine Bushnell's life and Butler's. Like Bushnell's, Butler's life centered on the crusade for social purity and the rescue of the "down-trodden mass of degraded womanhood." Butler sheltered sick and dying prostitutes in her guest room, frequently sending visiting friends to nearby hotels rather than turning the needy women out. She held many as they died and buried them in a cemetery near her home. She lectured publicly, and so incensed some of her listeners that she frequently had to leave quickly by the back door or window

---

1   F. L. Cross and E. A. Livingstone, eds., *The Oxford Dictionary of the Christian Church,* 2d ed. (New York: Oxford University Press, 1983), 215. Butler took Catherine of Siena as her model and wrote her biography, which was published in 1878.

2   John R. H. Moorman, *A History of the Church in England,* 3d ed. (London: Adam & Charles Black, 1976), 379.

35

of the lecture hall. On more than one occasion she was pursued by an angry mob that had "vowed to take her life."[3] Like Bushnell, Butler started reading rooms and houses where women who wished to escape prostitution could stay.

The particular focus of Butler's crusade was the repeal of the Contagious Diseases Acts, which the British Parliament had passed in 1865, 1867, and 1868. These acts "authorized a justice of the peace to detain a woman suspected of being a prostitute for examination and treatment. The claim of its advocates was that it prevented the spread of contagious diseases, but in reality it was for the protection of the men who visited the houses of ill-fame."[4] Associations were formed whose purpose was the abolition or the repeal of the acts: the male National Association for Repeal of the Acts, and the Ladies National Assocaition for Repeal, headed by Butler. Numerous branches throughout the country gathered signatures on petitions demanding repeal.[5]

Butler and William T. Stead,[6] a journalist, waged a campaign in 1882 against these Acts that brought about the appointment by the House of Commons of a committee to study the effect of the legislation. The committee's report was "that these Acts had neither checked disease nor promoted morality."[7] The acts were suspended in 1883 and repealed in 1886, but the suspicion remained that they were still being administered.

---

3 Kate C. Bushnell, "Mrs. Josephine Butler," *The Union Signal* 15 (26 December 1889), 10 (WCTU microfilm edition), roll 6, frame 107.

4 "Quick History of C. D. Acts," *The Union Signal* 20 (21 June 1894), 9 (WCTU microfilm edition), roll 9, frame 512.

5 Petrie, *Singular Iniquity,* 98.

6 Stead was most active in his attempts to get the age of consent for sexual activity raised to sixteen years, during which campaign he was imprisoned "upon the flimsiest technicality." During this imprisonment he wrote a life sketch of Josephine Butler (*The Inter Ocean,* 15 February 1886, photocopy).

7 Bushnell maintains that the chief force behind the abolition of the Contagious Diseases Acts was Butler, not Stead (Kate Bushnell, "An Appeal to Purity Workers," *The Union Signal* 20 [29 March 1894], 5 [WCTU microfilm edition], roll 9, frame 405).

On 17 June 1886 a memo was issued by the British Quarter-master-General of the Indian Government stating that "sufficient" attractive and properly medically inspected prostitutes were to be provided for the requirements of the men of the British army.[8] "Younger and more attractive native girls [were] to be put at the mercy of the British soldiers for the benefit of their health."[9] As this practice had been prohibited by the repeal of the Contagious Diseases Acts earlier that year, this memo made it obvious that the repeal was being ignored. In July 1886 a commission of the Free Church of Scotland discovered that the army had reopened and was regulating brothels near some of the military canton-ments in India. A copy of the "Infamous Memorandum" was sent to England from a "Christian gentleman" in India into whose hands it had fallen, and it was "reprinted and distributed to every member of the House of Commons." A furor ensued that ulti-mately resulted in the passage of a unanimous resolution in the House of Commons which stated that "any mere suspension of measures for the compulsory examination of women, and for licensing and regulation of prostitution in India, is insufficient; and the legislation which enjoins, authorizes, or permits such measures ought to be repealed."[10]

During this uproar, the Commander-in-Chief of the forces in India, Lord Roberts, wrote Butler, then secretary of the Interna-tional Abolitionist Federation, telling her that the reports were exaggerated,[11] although the federation had not requested from him such an assurance. This unsolicited denial and the conflict-ing reports that were received led the federation to undertake an investigation. Statistics were presented to the House of Com-mons showing that not only had venereal disease increased during the life of the acts, but also "that prostitution had become a state institution . . . even to the extreme of government-salaried

8 Elizabeth Andrew and Katharine Bushnell, *The Queen's Daughters in India* (London: Morgan & Scott, 1899), 18–19.

9 Bushnell, "Appeal to Purity Workers."

10 Andrew and Bushnell, *Queen's Daughters in India,* 21–22.

11 Petrie, *Singular Iniquity,* 266–67; Bell, *Flame of Fire,* 228–29; Arthur S. G. Butler, *Portrait of Josephine Butler* (London: Faber and Faber Ltd., 1954), 144.

brothel-keepers and procuresses."[12] Inquiry through official channels produced only denials, yet rumors continued to come to the ears of the federation. Its members were at a loss as how to proceed, however, because they lacked active leadership. Butler had become interested in the situation in India through a friend, Alfred Dyer, then living in Bombay, but the untimely death of Butler's husband left her "rendered inactive by grief."[13]

When Bushnell's letter arrived, it served to "arouse [Butler] from her inactive mourning."[14] Katharine Bushnell wrote, "I wish I had at hand a copy of the pamphlet Mrs. Butler wrote, in which she tells of the receipt of this letter, and of her first impulse to put it aside with only a casual glance."[15] She did not put it aside, however, and her reply to Bushnell stated that the federation had need of one or more women to go to India to tour the military cantonments and to "make careful inquiry into the condition of things there, with a view to ridding that people of the oppressive tyranny and shame imposed on them by Army authorities."[16]

While Katharine Bushnell had not met Josephine Butler, she was impressed by Butler's life and work and had written of it.[17] Bushnell showed her letter to Butler to a fellow member of the WCTU, Mrs. Elizabeth Andrew, who had been impressed with Stead's *Josephine Butler; a Life-Sketch.*[18] Bushnell and Andrew had been comissioned by Frances Willard and the other officers of the World WCTU to make a worldwide tour evangelizing in the interests of temperance and social purity.[19] Butler's plan was to fit the mission to India into their schedule,[20] although the work in India was to be done quietly and without the fanfare that they

---

12 Bushnell, "Appeal to Purity Workers."
13 Petrie, *Singular Iniquity,* 268. At this time both Butler's attention and the level of her interest failed, and she was still inactive a year later.
14 Ibid.
15 Bushnell, *Brief Sketch,* 9.
16 Butler, *Portrait,* 144; Petrie, *Singular Iniquity,* 267.
17 Bushnell, "Mrs. Josephine Butler."
18 Petrie, *Singular Iniquity,* 267.
19 Bushnell, *Brief Sketch,* 6.
20 Ibid., 12; Petrie, *Singular Iniquity,* 268.

hoped would attend the rest of their tour. Andrew agreed to join Bushnell in this endeavor also. As she had already booked passage to England, Andrew preceded Bushnell there, arriving in England before Bushnell had left her home in Evanston.[21]

Upon consenting to undertake the tour for the World WCTU, a fledgling organization with little or no financial base, both women had been told that they "could not expect the money for traveling expenses, or 'for so much as a postage stamp,'" and both had agreed to this condition. In order to finance her trip, Katharine Bushnell had set up a series of lecture engagements at stops along her way from Evanston to New York. Illness struck and disabled her voice before she had gotten as far as Ohio, forcing her to cancel a number of the engagements and to pile up hotel and medical bills during her recuperation, which wiped out all profits from her tour to this point. After prayer, she decided to go on, not knowing what the future held in the way of support. She arrived in New York City nearly penniless, without the means to purchase passage to England. However, she found in New York letters containing contributions that covered her expenses.[22]

At length, Bushnell joined Andrew in England; together they met with Josephine Butler, who explained the problem and the need in India. Butler felt that American women would arouse less suspicion than the two British male commissioners who had previously attempted to investigate the situation, and also that as a doctor, Bushnell might be granted admission to the hospitals, thereby gaining access to more information.[23]

Armed with a letter to "a confidential friend" in India who could be trusted to help them with the work, Bushnell and Andrew set sail from England in July 1891, making their first stop at Madeira, then proceeding to Capetown, South Africa, to speak for the World WCTU and to take up time until the hot summer months in India were past. They spent nearly six months in South Africa, and in December they left for India, going by way of

---

21 Bushnell, *Brief Sketch,* 12, 10.

22 Ibid., 6, 10–11. Bushnell said that this experience taught her a lesson she never forgot, and although she seldom charged for her services after that experience, God never failed to provide for her needs.

23 Ibid., 11.

Ceylon, where they rested for four days before beginning their confidential mission. Having met with great support from WCTU members all through South Africa, Andrew and Bushnell were apprehensive about what faced them in India, where the secret nature of their mission precluded either their taking the missionaries in India into their confidence or asking for their help.[24]

Bushnell and Andrew arrived in India at the end of December 1891 and met with the "confidential friend." This man sent them on to yet another friend who could acquaint them with the customs and conditions in the interior, and, in general, aid them in their mission. This second gentleman, however, proved anything but helpful and tried to dissuade them from continuing. He declared their mission "foolish and impracticable," and stated "from his long experience that it was utterly impossible for women to get at the truth."[25]

Alienated by this attitude on the part of their only source of aid and weighted down by the burden of the secrecy of their task, Andrew and Bushnell reported that they turned to God, the only help they had. After a day spent in prayer and fasting (an activity to which the women had frequent recourse in the months to come), they determined to continue their mission[26] but continued to run into obstacles and made no headway.

A visit to the chief military surgeon in charge of one of the cantonment hospitals on 4 January 1892 gained them little but official evasion. The surgeon deplored the repeal of the Acts and what he felt was the consequent increase in venereal disease, and he denied that there was any form of regulation or Lock Hospitals (where women were incarcerated during the duration of their disease). Andrew and Bushnell surmised that the surgeon "was endeavoring to mislead us."[27] Other attempts proved equally futile.

---

24 Andrew and Bushnell, *Queen's Daughters in India*, 25; *The Union Signal* 19 (2 November 1893), 5 (WCTU microfilm edition), roll 9, frame 206. Information given in a speech by Andrew at the WCTU Convention (Chicago, 1893).

25 Andrew and Bushnell, *Queen's Daughters in India*, 25.

26 Ibid., 26.

27 Ibid., 27.

For the next five weeks the women tried in vain to find some means of penetrating the barriers that separated them from information about regulated prostitution in India. At the end of the five weeks they were near despair, and once again spent the day in prayer. The resulting guidance led them to a friend who had lived in India for a considerable period of time. This friend instructed them in the language, manners, and "customs of the country, thus making us more independent in our work and travels."[28] This native knowledge also enabled Bushnell and Andrew to alter their approach to their investigations; they began to interview the women themselves and the native physicians and nurses who treated them.

Suddenly, through native cabmen and interpreters, Bushnell and Andrew found that they were able to gain access to the Lock Hospitals. The women reported that "in these Lock Hospitals we studied the annual reports for 1891, and books and records as far as possible, taking careful notes of everything important in interviews, records, etc., and drawing plans of several government houses of shame and Lock Hospitals."[29] They found that there was no suspicion attached to the party, and their inquiries proceeded apace. Their method was to walk into the house or hospital, hold a short service consisting of some songs sung in the native tongue by the interpreter, a short gospel message, and then the question, "Why are you in such a place as this?" In response to this question the stories would pour forth. Andrew and Bushnell were also able to speak to the *mahaldarnis* who procured, trained, and supervised the girls in the cantonments. They were able to purchase examples of the registration tickets given to the "clean" women after examination to prove that they were able to carry on their profession without contaminating the British soldiers. Often the women found that the younger prostitutes, some as young as eleven years, were the children of British soldiers, left behind when a soldier's tour of duty was over. Women who wished to give up prostitution were held to it by a

28 Ibid., 28.
29 Elizabeth Wheeler Andrew, "A Winter's Purity Campaign in India," *The Union Signal* 19 (11 May 1893), 2 (WCTU microfilm edition), roll 8, frame 578.

system of fines and also by the caste system which negated the possibility of their earning a living in any other way.[30] The evidence proving the military government's participation in the regulation of vice began to mount.

Once the information began to flow, the two women worked hard to record it. They spoke with

> over three hundred Cantonment women, held to prostitution by the iron law of military regulation, collected together by Government procuresses, who were used as the ultimate tools of the administration in carrying out . . . [the] military order for a sufficient number of attractive women, forced to the indecent exposure of their persons by misnamed "doctors," under penalty of fine or expulsion from the Cantonment, which was tantamount to starvation; imprisoned for several days of each month, even when in perfect health, in the Lock Hospital . . . often turned out when seriously diseased, with their British children, to starve, or to spread disease at will among the natives, the final scapegoats of British profligacy; dismissed to starvation when too old to be [any] longer "sufficiently attractive" to the soldier . . .

A typical journey would find Andrew and Bushnell traveling as "intermediate" passengers in the trains to avoid attracting attention as first- or second-class passengers, arriving at their destinations in the middle of the night, sleeping in the ladies' waiting rooms at the train stations, and eating in station refreshment-rooms. They would hire a driver, who would frequently object to taking them into the cantonment prostitution district. They would then hold their service, listen to the stories of the women, talk to any supervisory personnel to whom they could gain access, and return to the train station to leave for their next destination. When asked how they managed to avoid confrontation with military authorities, they replied, "We can only say that we made but little effort on our own part to do this, and trusted the Lord to do it all for us."[31] During the first three months of 1892,

---

30 Andrew and Bushnell, *Queen's Daughters in India,* 31–32, 52, 42.

31 Ibid., 42 (the lengthy quote comes from this page), 30–31, 45–53, 48.

Katharine Bushnell and Elizabeth Andrew visited ten cantonments, five of which they visited twice.[32]

At length Bushnell and Andrew completed their studies and spent three weeks in Calcutta compiling their report,[33] which they sent back to Josephine Butler and the federation in England. Their statistics were impressive: more than thirty-six hundred miles traveled, ten military stations visited, 395 prostitutes interviewed in addition to Lock Hospital medical personnel and patients and others.[34] Having accomplished this part of their mission, they continued on their world tour for the World WCTU, holding public meetings in the countries of Australia and New Zealand. About their business in India, they were warned by cable, "Silence concerning India imperative," and shortly thereafter were recalled to England to appear before a committee appointed by Lord Kimberly at the request of Prime Minister Gladstone, who had read their confidential report and was "simply horrified."[35]

Things in England then became quite lively, with accusations and denials flying back and forth. Lord Roberts had returned to England in April of 1893, having been succeeded in India as Commander-in-Chief by Sir George White.[36] Bushnell's and Andrew's report appeared in the newspapers, followed by Lord Roberts's denial. Newspapers characterized the two women as well-intentioned but ill-informed philanthropists.[37] Nonetheless, governmental investigations ensued, and the report came back from India that the women's allegations were true. The Indian military officials had, when the Contagious Diseases Acts were repealed, "set to work to collect evidence from year to year to show the great increase in disease in consequence of this compulsory repeal of the Acts in India." News of the statistics sub-

---

32 Ibid., 29; Andrew, "Winter's Purity Campaign."

33 *The Union Signal* 19 (2 November 1893), 5 (WCTU microfilm edition), roll 9, frame 206. Report of Elizabeth Andrew's speech delivered to the WCTU Convention, Chicago, 1893.

34 Andrew, "Winter's Purity Campaign."

35 Bushnell, *Brief Sketch*, 13.

36 Butler, *Portrait*, 145.

37 Bell, *Flame of Fire*, 231.

stantiating this increase had already been published in medical journals in India and in British military papers, and so could not be covered up. This statistical evidence had been collected during the period of the repeal to prove the efficacy of the Contagious Diseases Acts in controlling disease. The report of Bushnell and Andrew showed that regulation and compulsory examination had never ceased, and therefore the reported increase in venereal disease had occurred during regulation. The commission sent to India for the records that had been kept to prove the increase of the disease, and this was prima facie evidence of the truth of the women's accusations.[38]

Called before the department commission in August 1893, Lord Roberts denied knowledge of the "Infamous Memorandum" distributed in his name in 1886. In a letter to her son, Josephine Butler describes the hearing:

> I attended yesterday a Committee in Westminster about Lord Roberts's denial, etc. . . . Things are rather lively at present, with Lord Roberts's hard swearing and our flat assertions. . . . Lord Roberts sent for Stead two days ago, to make a statement for him to give out to the world. . . . Stead wrote to me some of their conversation. Lord Roberts abused us rather. Stead said to him, "Well, let us understand each other. You think us fanatics, fools, hysterical people. Very good. We think you and your set the children of the Devil, who are working to bring his kingdom on earth . . . " Lord Roberts: " . . . I maintain that the facts are not as you state. No such regulation has existed since 1888."[39]

Lord Roberts continued to deny the practice of regulation, saying he would have known of it, and that any of his men who did practice regulation should be "broken, decidedly, every one of them. For they would be guilty of insubordination in the highest degree." Butler continues, "You see how good Lord

---

38 Bushnell, "Appeal to Purity Workers." The Indian medical journals mentioned by Bushnell were the *Medical Journal* of Calcutta and the *Gazette* of India.
39 Butler, *Portrait,* 146.

Roberts's attitude is for us. It will tend to bring the guilt home to the really guilty people, and our case will be fully proved."[40]

Lord Roberts's quartermaster, General Chapman, who was immediately responsible for the memorandum, was also called. Butler describes his testimony:

> Then came [Lord Roberts's] betrayer for examination before the Commission. Chapman . . . is a dark, evil-looking man, lean, dried up like a piece of old tree trunk, expressionless, with a mouth of a peculiar form—thin, mechanical, which slowly opens like a steel trap to emit the lies he speaks with a face of black night and imperturbable impenitence—then shuts again, like a skeleton's mouth.
>
> Asked by Stansfeld if he had a distinct order from Lord Roberts to draw up that circular, the mouth opened, said "Certainly" and clanked shut again.
>
> "Did Lord Roberts initiate it?" "Certainly."
>
> "Did Lord Roberts see it in proof and read it over?" "Most certainly. He read it over and entirely approved it."
>
> George Russell (Chairman) and all the questioners, including General Stewart who began by being ferociously against us, leaned back in silence, shocked and, as it were, sickened by the strangeness of the situation.[41]

The commission's subsequent report stated "that there 'appeared to be a discrepancy' in the evidence on this point," a statement that infuriated Butler.[42] In a letter to be included with the report, Lord Roberts allowed that he felt the women were due an apology, which he forthwith offered.[43] However, he also stated that he felt the women would have been better off and saved much unpleasantness had they "commended themselves to the

---

40 Ibid.
41 Ibid., 147.
42 Bell, *Flame of Fire,* 232.
43 Andrew and Bushnell, *Queen's Daughters in India,* 95–96; Bushnell, "Appeal to Purity Workers."

care of the authorities in India."[44] The newspapers were quick to point out that if they had, there would have been no report.[45] Member of Parliament James Stansfeld said that "he had never, in the course of his long public career, seen a piece of work so well done, so carefully, skillfully and courageously carried through to the end, to be crowned with the success it deserved. No *man* or set of men . . . could possibly have done it so well."[46]

Bushnell and Andrew continued their round-the-world campaign in the interests of social purity. On 22 April 1892 they sailed from Bombay for Ceylon, en route to Melbourne, Australia, where they arrived on 13 May to begin a tour that lasted about five months.[47] October found them on board ship again, sailing from Sydney to Auckland, New Zealand, where they joined in the fight against New Zealand's Contagious Diseases Acts. In February 1893, they were called back to England to be the chief speakers at the International Congress for Men and Women in May and the World's Temperance Congress in June.[48] They spoke about their work in India, the places they had been, and the women with whom they had spoken. However, they were not "at liberty to talk of the [contents of the report] until the report of the department committee of Parliament had been made."[49]

On 24 August, Bushnell and Andrew were honored at a party in London at which they received from Stansfeld "a handsome gift of money and an illuminated address, expressing for himself and the British Committee the warmest appreciation and grati-

44 Ibid.; "The Outcome of a Noble Work," *The Union Signal* 19 (5 October 1893), 9 (WCTU microfilm edition), roll 9, frame 171.

45 Ibid.; Andrew and Bushnell, *Queen's Daughters in India,* 92.

46 *The Union Signal* 19 (2 November 1893), 4 (WCTU microfilm edition), roll 9, frame 206. From a letter from Josephine Butler read at the WCTU Convention in Chicago, 1893.

47 *The Union Signal* 18 (8 December 1892), 1 (WCTU microfilm edition), roll 8, frame 359.

48 Sharing the platform with them at the International Congress were such notables as Drs. Elizabeth and Emily Blackwell, Susan B. Anthony, Julia Ward Howe, Josephine Butler, William T. Stead, Lady Henry Somerset, and others ("Outcome of a Noble Work").

49 Ibid.

tude for their services. . . ."[50] On 26 August, they boarded the steamship *Paris* at Southampton. They were bound for the United States and the World WCTU convention to be held in Chicago in October.

In September, Andrew and Bushnell received an official cablegram from England telling them of the full vindication of their allegations and of the letter of apology written by Lord Roberts. Although they had known of this before they left England, they had been unable to speak of it because of the continued secrecy of the investigations.[51]

In the end, Lord Roberts was issued a severe reprimand, Bushnell and Andrew were paid eight hundred pounds in reimbursement for their Indian expenses, and the regulations were amended. But the fight was not over. Almost immediately associations sprang up whose sole purpose was to reinstate regulation. The Anglo-Indian press prophesied:

> The religious fanatics who howled until a weak Government gave way to their clamour will probably howl again now at the way the old order of things will be enforced under another name but with very little difference in manner. The way the Indian Government have got over the difficulty is simply by classing venereal diseases in the same category as small-pox and other contagious diseases which the law provides for by segregation, special hospitals, etc. . . . The new rules are the work of a master in the art of making a thing look as unlike itself as it well can be.[52]

By 1897, the practice of semi-official regulated prostitution had been resumed as a weapon for the control of venereal disease.[53] However, by this time Katharine Bushnell was back in the United States and involved in her Bible studies there.

---

50   *The Union Signal* 19 (14 September 1893), 5 (WCTU microfilm edition), roll 9, frame 140.

51   *The Union Signal* 19 (21 September 1893), 1 (WCTU microfilm edition), roll 9, frame 146.

52   Petrie, *Singular Iniquity,* 269.

53   Ibid.; Bell, *Flame of Fire,* 228.

RETURN TO CHINA:
OPIUM AND FORCED PROSTITUTION

※

A t the request of Lady Henry Somerset and Frances Willard, Bushnell and Andrew returned reluctantly to the United States in early September 1893. Although they had been scheduled to return to India and continue on to China and Japan, "their presence and consecrated zeal were of too much value to be missed from our great meetings this autumn [the World WCTU Convention in Chicago]."[1] The statistics of their work to this point in their travels are impressive: They had been out of the country for over two years, during which time they had

> traveled eighty-seven thousand miles, making sixteen sea voyages on twenty-six different bodies of water, and crossing the equator four times. During this period they have given six hundred and seventy addresses to forty-five thousand people, speaking in England, Wales, Cape Colony, Natal, Orange Free State, the Transvaal, India, Ceylon, Victoria, South Australia, Queensland, New South Wales, New Zealand, Tasmania, Egypt and Palestine.[2]

Their stay in the United States was not lengthy. After speaking at the convention, Bushnell and Andrew sailed for England

---

1 *The Union Signal* 19 (2 November 1893), 3 (WCTU microfilm edition), roll 9, frame 204.

2 *The Union Signal* 19 (4 May 1893), 10 (WCTU microfilm edition), roll 2, frame 65.

on 8 November.[3] The voyage was difficult and they rested a few days with friends in London, spent a few days more at Lady Henry Somerset's Reigate estate,[4] and then continued their interrupted journey back to India and on to Burma, China, and Japan. This time their intended purpose was not secret inquiry, but open crusade for social purity. In Bombay, however, Bushnell and Andrew received yet another plea for help from yet another reforming group in England.

As the excitement from the exposure of the extent of government regulation of vice in India abated, a new concern was coming to the attention of the reformers. A group opposed to the opium trade had generated enough apprehension throughout England to have a Royal Commission appointed to investigate that trade. However, the groups in favor of abolition of the opium trade feared that "the evidence [the commission] has collected—rather, the *opinions* it has compiled, will . . . support the opium traffic as much as possible."[5] There were rumors of officials in high places with heavy interest and involvement in the trade, including the commission's chair, who "was believed to own large opium estates in the Orient."[6] British medical personnel stationed in India to treat European residents there testified that in their many years of experience in the East they had "never seen any traces of the evil effects of opium," and other witnesses alluded to its efficacy as "sharpener of the wits" and "queller of mutiny." A majority of those serving on the commission also favored the trade, and "the impression was given, in its [initial] report, that opium was beneficial to its users."[7]

---

3 *The Union Signal* 19 (2 November 1893), 3 (WCTU microfilm edition), roll 9, frame 204; 19 (30 November 1893), 1 (WCTU microfilm edition), roll 9, frame 255.

4 *The Union Signal* 19 (18 December 1893), 1 (WCTU microfilm edition), roll 9, frame 288.

5 "Our Third and Fourth Round-the-World Missionaries in the Orient," *The Union Signal* 20 (16 August 1894), 4 (WCTU microfilm edition), roll 9, frame 561.

6 Bushnell, *Brief Sketch,* 18.

7 "Missionaries in the Orient," *The Union Signal* 20 (16 August 1894).

Not satisfied with this report, an anti-opium organization requested that Bushnell and Andrew look into the state of affairs in the Orient and report on the extent of the trade and the effects of opium on its users. As their round-the-world tour continued, they became increasingly aware of the dual attitude toward opium. Forces in favor of continuing and supporting the trade seemed as strong as those in favor of abolition. In a report to *The Union Signal*, Bushnell and Andrew predicted "there will be a great battle on in England this winter." This opinion was also held by those in England, for when Bushnell and Andrew reached Bombay they were asked to consider returning to England to help fight for the abolition after the final report was made to Parliament. They promised to pray about the request and to follow the Lord's leading.[8]

As they "were going directly to opium-cursed regions," the women did feel led "to study the extent of the evils of opium smoking"[9] in addition to their regular duties of holding meetings and helping to reorganize the WCTU chapters in the cities they visited. In their investigations they went into opium dens where the smoking of opium was the only activity, and into other places such as brothels where opium was habitually used. Most of the brothels had a couch or small room near the entrance that was hung with pipes and other paraphernalia for the smoking of opium.[10] Food, drink, and opium could be ordered by patrons at will. Bushnell and Andrew interviewed opium users who testified as to the "destruction of character wrought upon them by its use," and compiled "an abundance of evidence that opium fed the social vice [prostitution], and that the two went hand in hand."[11] Bushnell blamed the profusion of the trade on the British and the Americans, who excused themselves by saying the Orientals preferred the opium trade to continue. Bushnell vehemently disagreed wih these excuses: "We have never known man, woman or child in India, Burmah [sic] or China, whether victims

8 Bushnell, *Brief Sketch*, 18.
9 Ibid.
10 Elizabeth Andrew and Katharine Bushnell, *Heathen Slaves and Christian Rulers* (Oakland, CA: Messiah's Advocate, 1907), 121, 128.
11 Bushnell, *Brief Sketch*, 19.

of the drug or not, among the Orientalists [sic] who had a good word to say of opium, and personally know that the opinions and the experiences of many are, of course, exactly to the contrary."[12]

Bushnell acknowledged that there was a criminal element in Oriental society that did encourage the use of opium, and as an example she describes the horror of a Chinese parade celebrating the rededication of a Buddhist temple: Painted prostitutes rode on bullocks with their "pocket-mothers" (owners) beside them, watching over them and keeping on the lookout for business.

> Yet more painful was the sight of little girls, bound with heavy wires and placed in all manner of contortion . . . wired into the distressing shape they occupied, and it was said that none of them could have endured the position but for plentiful doses of opium.[13]

In this particular celebration, the British joined not only with their presence but also with speeches of congratulation.[14]

The British government itself was interested in another kind of trade then flourishing around Singapore and Hong Kong. Chinese women and girls were being sold to prostitution organizations in Hong Kong, Shanghai, and San Francisco, and the Marquis of Ripon, England's Colonial Secretary, was interested in "strengthening the law of those regions for the protection of women and girls."[15] In their research into the opium question, Bushnell and Andrew were requested to investigate forced prostitution as well, and preferably, as in their investigations in India, without drawing public attention to what they were doing.

As in India, Bushnell and Andrew met nothing but evasion and outright lying from the Protectors[16] and their staffs. These

---

12 "Missionaries in the Orient," *The Union Signal* 20 (16 August 1894).
13 Andrew and Bushnell, *Heathen Slaves and Christian Rulers*, 125–26.
14 Ibid., 126.
15 Bushnell, *Brief Sketch*, 19.
16 The title "Protector of the Chinese" was given to the official (later called the Registrar General) who was charged with the protection of Chinese slaves who were diseased and/or wished to be freed from their owners. This official was also charged with the enforcement

officials denied that there were Lock Hospitals, but Bushnell and Andrew had visited a Lock Hospital in which they found equipment only for the purpose of pelvic examinations and for the treatment of venereal disease; the hospital housed fifteen prostitutes but no other patients at the time of their visit. The officials assured the women that there was no government-required examination, but Andrew and Bushnell had "dozens of papers of commitment to the Lock Hospitals for compulsory examination." The Protector was to have nothing to do with procurement for the brothels, but was to rescue girls from them; yet the records examined by Bushnell showed that in 1893, "1183 girls entered the brothels with the sanction of the Protector."[17] The prostitutes were given "tickets" purportedly for their use in seeking help from the Protector to claim their freedom should they desire it. Few, if any, of the women could read, however, and the promises on the tickets were sometimes printed illegibly.

Bushnell and Andrew were assured that the law specified that no girl under the age of sixteen was permitted on the premises of a brothel, and that violation of this law by the brothel operator was punishable by a year in prison or a five-hundred-dollar fine. They were repeatedly assured that this law, above all others, was obeyed to the letter.[18] The missionaries were completely shattered when their investigation revealed that because of their inquiries "a handful" of little girls under eight years of age had been taken from the brothel where they were being trained to a future life of prostitution and sent to the Lock Hospital for

---

of the 1857 ordinance that specified that slavery was illegal (declared so in the Queen's Anti-Slavery Proclamation of 1845) and that the government had a duty to provide free medical care to any sick or former slaves (Andrew and Bushnell, *Heathen Slaves and Christian Rulers*, 13–15).

17 Ibid., 131–33, 134.

18 Ibid., 6–9. One way of avoiding this law was the use of "Tanka" women and girls in the slave trade. These women were not considered to be Hong Kong citizens, but "river people" of no particular citizenship. These "Tanka" sold their female relatives, their own female children, and female children they had kidnapped in mainland China into slavery in Hong Kong to be trained as prostitutes.

compulsory examination. These young children were returned to the brothels because it was found that they were still virgins! The Protectorate, which had ordered the compulsory examination of the little girls, would do nothing until they were "deflowered," and refused to take action of any kind to see that this did not happen.[19]

Bushnell was appalled at the complaisance toward forced prostitution that she found among the British government officials in China. In this she was joined by Chinese Christians, who were amazed at the level of participation by "Englishmen and Americans who called themselves 'Christians.'"[20] Men publicly recognized for their acts of Christian charity were the authors of ordinances punishing Chinese women who attempted to leave the owners who forced them to work as prostitutes.[21] Bushnell felt that the Christian nations were judged by the morals of the men who came to the Orient and set up the system of brothel slavery, domestic slavery, and coolie labor.[22] The fact that children as young as seven were kept in training in opium dens and houses of prostitution, and that the "Christian"[23] officers of the Protectorate would do nothing to secure the children's release,[24] was an utter condemnation of Christianity as far as the Chinese were concerned.[25]

---

19 Ibid., 137–39.
20 Ibid., 126.
21 According to Bushnell, Sir John Bowring, British consul and Superintendent of Trade in Canton (1849), later Governor of Hong Kong (1854) and writer of the hymns "Watchman, Tell Us of the Night" and "In the Cross of Christ I Glory," was one originator of such legislation. Bushnell, *Brief Sketch*, 21; Andrew and Bushnell, *Heathen Slaves and Christian Rulers*, 12–13.
22 Ibid., II.
23 In the preface of *Heathen Slaves and Christian Rulers*, Andrew and Bushnell explain that they are using the word "Christian" to mean those raised in countries where Christianity was the norm and who had not disavowed Christianity for another religion (I).
24 Bushnell, *Brief Sketch*, 20–22.
25 It was only after Bushnell and Andrew returned to the United States that the full story of their investigations in Hong Kong was written and published as *Heathen Slaves and Christian Rulers* (1907).

Bushnell and Andrew presented their written report to the Colonial Secretary in person and were later notified of the results of their efforts by the Colonial Office. Bushnell's strong feelings about the degradation of women in China who were forced into prostitution are well expressed in her statement that "one 'Protector' of the girls, at least, was retired from his lofty official position and went into business in London more in keeping with his station—he opened a cigar stand."[26]

Bushnell and Andrew continued their round-the-world trip for the World WCTU, traveling further in China, Australia, and Japan. They were in Hong Kong in February, and on 8 March 1894 they reached Shanghai, where Bushnell saw for the first time in twelve years the mission field she had left in sorrow and what she had previously felt to be abject failure. She visited the old familiar places of her mission work and was even met by one of her former Chinese friends, a Kiukiang tailor.[27] She was moved by her homecoming and enjoyed her return to Kiukiang, where she and Andrew gave talks and worked with the WCTU.

In most places in China Bushnell and Andrew were well received; however, they did on occasion meet with some hostility. In Tien-Tsin, after reorganizing the WCTU chapter, Bushnell spoke to a nearly all-male audience who had come to hear her talk about social purity, an audience whose main expectations were of "some coarse, low fun. She looked them calmly in the face and with that deep, spiritual power, before which all base things cower, talked directly to them of God's punishment until they must have felt the judgement day had come."[28]

The stay in Japan was cut short. The women were weary and felt that God was guiding them to leave early.[29] They were also worried by the threat of plague and feared that they would be caught in the impending outbreak. They stopped their tour

---

26 Bushnell, *Brief Sketch*, 19.

27 "Our Third and Fourth Round-the-World Missionaries in the Orient," *The Union Signal* 20 (23 August 1894).

28 *The Union Signal* 20 (7 June 1894), 1 (WCTU microfilm edition), roll 9, frame 489.

29 *The Union Signal* 20 (5 July 1894), 1 (WCTU microfilm edition), roll 9, frame 524.

abruptly and from Yokohama set sail for the United States in the ship *S.S. Oceana*.[30] They arrived in San Francisco on 18 June, two weeks before they were expected. However, rest was not to be granted to them yet. Immediately upon docking, they were met with urgent cables calling them back to England. The Royal Opium Commission was about to report to Parliament, and the "matter of the state regulation of vice in India" was surfacing again. With "scarcely an hour's rest," they boarded another ship headed for England so they could attend the July meetings in London of the British, Continental and General Federation for the Abolition of the State Regulation of Vice.[31] That they were barely able to catch the only ship that could get them to the meetings on time convinced both Andrew and Bushnell that it was indeed the Lord's leading that had brought them home early. Newspaper articles had given the impression that they had returned due to the threat of the plague. Bushnell denied this, explaining that

> There is no plague as yet in Japan, but it is feared, and all outgoing and incoming vessels were being strictly watched, and a quarantine was so imminent that we thought it best to come home a little earlier than we had planned, and realize now that, as we were all along impressed, it was the Lord's leading.[32]

On their return to England, Bushnell and Andrew were actively engaged in traveling about the country, meeting with interested groups and telling the story of their experiences. Bushnell had long since concluded that changing the laws would accomplish little unless the facts and terrible details of the problems were laid before all of the people, generating an interest in the righting of wrongs.[33] To this end she and Andrew devoted their

---

30 *The Union Signal* 20 (14 June 1894), 1 (WCTU microfilm edition), roll 9, frame 497.

31 *The Union Signal* 20 (5 July 1894), 1 (WCTU microfilm edition), roll 9, frame 529.

32 *The Union Signal* 20 (9 August 1894), 9 (WCTU microfilm edition), roll 9, frame 555. Report of a trans-Atlantic phone call from Bushnell and Andrew to *The Union Signal* offices.

33 Bushnell, *Brief Sketch*, 19.

time and energy for the remainder of their time in England, working with the English Social Purity section of the WCTU, which was ably headed by Jospehine Butler. Of Butler, Bushnell wrote, "She penetrated with deeper insight into the problems of the social evil than any woman who ever lived."[34]

Bushnell and Andrew were expected to return to the United States by October of 1894,[35] but their stay stretched on into the spring of 1895. Under the sponsorship and leadership of Lady Henry Somerset, a series of twenty meetings was held "in the great commercial centers of Great Britain,"[36] the finale of which was a "great anti-opium demonstration" held in Queen's Hall, London, on 22 March 1895. These meetings immediately preceded the release of the contents of the report of the Royal Opium Commission, which was still expected to be favorable to the opium trade. The anti-opium force believed, however, that "whatever the commission may report nothing can alter the facts or successfully dispute the evidence given by Mrs. Andrew and Dr. Bushnell."[37] Every meeting at which they spoke passed resolutions against the opium trade, resolutions that were sent on to the Prime Minister, Secretary of State for Foreign Affairs, and members of the House of Commons.

Their long anti-opium campaign over, Bushnell and Andrew retired to a chalet in Switzerland for several weeks of rest. Butler, who was ill, stayed for a week at a nearby hotel, joining them during the day for rest, talk, and prayer.[38] During their stay, Bushnell and Andrew were recommissioned as round-the-world missionaries.[39]

---

34 Ibid., 22.
35 *The Union Signal* 20 (5 July 1894), 1 (WCTU microfilm edition), roll 9, frame 524.
36 *The Union Signal* 21 (11 April 1895), 4, 16 (WCTU microfilm edition), roll 10, frame 242; Henry J. Osborn, "Close of the Anti-Opium Campaign in England," *The Union Signal* 21 (18 April 1895), 4 (WCTU microfilm edition), roll 10, frame 250.
37 Osborn, "Close of the Anti-Opium Campaign."
38 Bushnell, *Brief Sketch*, 17.
39 *The Union Signal* 21 (1 August 1895), 1 (WCTU microfilm edition), roll 10, frame 363.

They remained at the chalet through August, then went on to continue the introduction of purity work throughout Europe.[40]

In December 1895, with both women exhausted and Andrew ill, Bushnell and Andrew returned to the United States. They rested for seven weeks at the Battle Creek (Michigan) Sanitarium, after which they went on to Andrew's home in Rochester, New York.[41] Andrew was still recovering from their long and wearing journeys, but Bushnell made herself available for lecturing once more, making Andrew's home her headquarters. Then, when Andrew regained her strength, she and Bushnell returned to their roles as round-the-world missionaries and set off once again.

Back on the road, Bushnell and Andrew worked again in Australia.[42] In the spring of 1897 they were in South Africa, helping women there understand the implications and the procedures surrounding the Contagious Diseases Acts that were about to be enacted in that country.[43] Finally, they returned once more to England, where they continued to speak and hold meetings, trying desperately to combat the reinstitution of the Contagious Disease Acts.[44]

---

40 *The Union Signal* 21 (11 April 1895), 4 (microfilm edition), roll 10, frame 242.
41 *The Union Signal* 22 (26 March 1896), 11 (WCTU microfilm edition), roll 11, frame 030.
42 *The Union Signal* 22 (26 November 1896), 12 (WCTU microfilm edition), roll 11, frame 304; (17 December 1896), roll 11, frame 334.
43 *The Union Signal* 22 (25 March 1896), 10 (WCTU microfilm edition), roll 11, frame 452.
44 Bushnell, *Brief Sketch*, 22.

END OF AN ERA

🙰

The specter of government regulation of prostitution in India would not be put to rest, even after the repeal in 1895 of the Contagious Diseases Acts. The party in favor of continued regulation of prostitution was unceasing in its determination to have the acts reinstituted. The incidence of venereal disease continued to be reported as rising.

In April 1896, Lord Roberts and his constituents organized an association for the promotion of new Contagious Diseases Acts, and this group appeared before Parliament to plead for the acts' passage.[1] One year later, the association received unexpected and—as far as the temperance and purity forces were concerned—shocking support from Lady Henry Somerset, president of the British Women's Temperance Association and vice president of the World WCTU, who appeared to be reversing her former stance on the issue of social purity. Inasmuch as the clash between Bushnell and Lady Henry[2] over this apparent reversal signaled the beginning of the end of Bushnell's association with the world and national WCTUs, it is well to say something more about Lady Henry Somerset's life and involvement in the temperance and social purity movements.

---

1 *The Union Signal* 22 (29 April 1896), 8 (WCTU microfilm edition), roll 11, frame 492.
2 Although it may appear strange to modern American eyes, the appellation "Lady Henry" is the proper title for the wife of a younger son of a duke.

Isabella Somers Cocks (1851–1921) was born in London to an aristocratic and overprotective family.[3] Until she married at twenty years of age, Isabella's mother kept her "unspoiled and unconscious of her attractions," but also "ignorant of life." Isabella was obsessed with the idea of being "really good," an obsession somewhat at odds with her "gay, warm-hearted, beauty-loving and pleasure-loving nature."[4] She eventually accepted the proposal of Lord Henry Somerset, second son of the Duke of Beaufort, who had assured her that he shared this desire to "be good." In 1872 they married, and they lived at Badminton. The marriage soon became abusive. After the birth of one child, in 1878, they entered into a permanent separation, as Lady Henry could not bear the notoriety of divorce.[5] Lord Henry had been so brutal that the child, a son, was left in Lady Henry's custody—a circumstance nearly unheard of in a time when the common law stated that "the father is guardian by nature and by nurture and his rights are to be considered primary."[6]

Although the separation was not her fault, Lady Henry was still ostracized by society, and at her father's death in 1883 she retired to her Reigate estate, where she spent the next seven years. There she became involved with a nearby group of Methodists and began to work among the poor and oppressed. She was soon part of the temperance movement, which was not popular among her social peers. She was rebuked from the pulpit by a curate for her "impudence," and called a "traitor to her class" by a neighboring aristocrat.[7]

In 1889 Lady Henry came under the influence of Hannah Whitall Smith,[8] who persuaded her to become president of the British Women's Temperance Association (BWTA). In October 1891 Smith took Lady Henry to America, where she gained instant

3 Kathleen Fitzpatrick, *Lady Henry Somerset* (Boston: Little, Brown, and Company, 1923), chap. 1.
4 Ibid., 93, 1.
5 Ibid., 97–118.
6 Ibid., 110.
7 Ibid., 147–48.
8 Hannah Whitall Smith was author of *The Christian's Secret of a Happy Life.*

popularity as a speaker. She remained through the winter, becoming a close friend of Frances Willard, and returned to England in April 1892.

Lady Henry was not a prohibitionist. She supported temperance and was a part of the BWTA because liquor "had become a tyranny that forced men to be drunkards; but she believed that, if the claws of the Trade were cut and men were set free to be sober, wine-drinking might be as innocent a pleasure in England and America as it is in Italy and France."[9] Lady Henry herself was fond an occasional glass of wine and it was with difficulty that she persuaded herself to "take the pledge," doing so primarily as an example.

The social purity section of the World WCTU had never been Lady Henry Somerset's particular interest. "She had always declared herself entirely unwilling to study or even to hear anything about questions of morality, regarding the subject as unsavoury."[10] She felt that the purity question should be left to those "who had a taste for it." And according to her biographer, the "trouble with [Bushnell and Andrew] was that they did have a taste for it."[11] Lady Henry, however, had been most supportive of the efforts of Butler, Bushnell, and Andrew in the social purity section of the World WCTU. Bushnell and Andrew had carried on a correspondence with Lady Henry Somerset during their 1892 tour as round-the-world missionaries. They had visited her home at Eastnor,[12] and she had financially sponsored and led them in the anti-opium campaign in England and the Orient in early 1895.

Therefore, when propositions in favor of regulation of prostitution and rules for examination of both men and women were suggested by Lady Henry, the ensuing furor raged on both sides of the Atlantic. On 26 March 1897 the *Times* had published Lord George Hamilton's dispatch containing six propositions regarding regulation.[13] Hamilton, Secretary of State for India, had sent

---

9   Fitzpatrick, *Lady Henry Somerset,* 184.

10 Bell, *Flame of Fire,* 288.

11 Ibid., 191.

12 *The Union Signal* 19 (18 December 1893), 1 (WCTU microfilm edition), roll 9, frame 288.

13 Henry J. Wilson, *A Rough Record of Events and Incidents Connected*

Lady Henry a copy of his proposed policy, and requested that she write him a letter on this subject. She did this, and on 21 April 1897, her letter was printed in the *Times*.[14]

This about-face was even more surprising, given the fact that earlier that month the BWTA, at its annual council meeting, had unanimously adopted a resolution declaring its strong opposition to re-enacting any semblance of the Contagious Diseases Acts in India, and encouraged that efforts be made instead to solve the problem of immorality and venereal disease by moral methods. A protest signed by a number of bishops' wives, Josephine Butler, and other well-known women was sent to the government.[15] The BWTA also emphatically objected to any kind of regulation that would require the examination and registration of women for the purposes of supplying women for the use of the men in the British Army. However, Lady Henry felt she was writing as an individual and expressing her own views, not those of her associates in the temperance and social purity movements.[16]

In her letter, Lady Henry made some suggestions for the carrying out of Hamilton's suggested measures for "Checking the Spread of Venereal Diseases among the British Troops in India." In addition, she commended Hamilton for ordering that "nothing should be done that can be represented as an encouragement to vice," and his recognition of the "paramount importance of raising the moral tone of the Indian Army." She supported the device of "including this disease in the category of other contagious diseases [such as smallpox]," and felt that this indicated "the only rational and scientific principle on which its eradication can be attempted."[17] Her principal concern was the failure of the acts

with the Repeal of the "Contagious Diseases Act, 1864–6–9" in the United Kingdom and of the Movement Against State Regulation of Vice in India and the Colonies, 1858-1906 (Sheffield, England: Parker Bros., 1907), no. 844.

14 Fitzpatrick, *Lady Henry Somerset,* 197–99.
15 Wilson, *Rough Record,* no. 828a.
16 *Leeds Mercury Journal,* April 1997. From Willard Scrapbook.
17 Fitzpatrick, *Lady Henry Somerset,* 197–200.

to address the moral issue explicitly. She saw the Contagious Diseases Acts as

> in reality as little concerned with the extirpation of the disease as with the inculcation of good morals. . . . The old system sought to guard the men against contagion by women. It did nothing to guard the women against contagion by the men. Make your system relentlessly strict as far as preventing any diseased person of either sex from poisoning another, and you will have done the only thing that is scientifically defensible; while the publicity, discipline and supervision it must imply, may prove one of the most effective moral safeguards that can be devised.[18]

To accomplish this Lady Henry suggested the examination not only of women, but also of men; the latter had been an unheard-of indignity. She suggested that identities of the infected soldiers were to be made public, and promotion tied to morality. On 26 May, she issued a pamphlet setting forth her proposals, described by one of her opponents as proposing "a peculiarly offensive form of Regulation."[19]

But then, not content to speak as an individual, Lady Henry used her influence as president of the BWTA and first vice president of the World WCTU to attempt to persuade members of local branches not to sign petitions opposing reinstatement of the acts.[20] All of the British branches of the BWTA refused to comply, and on 24 July 1897, Lady Henry resigned as president of the association in response to their denial of her request.

The resignation did not stand. In enthusiastic support of her leadership, three-fourths of the executive committee of the BWTA, made up of one hundred women from all parts of Britain, asked Lady Henry to stay, and she agreed to do so. To be sure, Lady Henry was not alone in her views. Statistics had been published that caused near panic "among persons who were not

---

18   Ibid., 200.
19   Wilson, *Rough Record*, no. 857.
20   "Defer to Lady Henry," *Chicago Times-Herald*, 1 August 1897; "Displeased with Lady Henry," *Kansas City Star*, 8 January 1889. Both articles from Willard Scrapbook.

accustomed to study statistics, and did not therefore realise that figures relating to a few years may often deceive. . . ."[21] A committee was appointed by the India Office to study the question. One hundred and twenty women, among them members of royalty and of the peerage, signed a "memorial [sic] praying for the re-introduction of regulation in India."[22]

This petition brought Josephine Butler out of retirement and back into immediate leadership of the International Abolitionist Federation, whose purpose was to abolish regulation. Reacting strongly against the petition, she wrote:

> . . . my heart is wounded with a sense of shame, and I mourn for those whose eyes are blinded to the truth . . . we cannot now, without the constant acting of a lie, pretend that we are now a united womanhood. Our cause will receive deeper wounds than it has ever received yet if we attempt to minimize or gloss over the hideous fact that women, ladies of high estate and honourable names, have publicly petitioned for the re-establishment in a portion of the British Empire of the master-piece of Satan, that 'covenant with death and agreement with hell'! . . . Our race is suffering largely from a species of moral atrophy, from a fatal paralysis of the sense of justice. Many literally do not know what justice is. . . . The poor cannot so easily forget the real meaning of Justice: they are reminded of what Justice is, too often, by its absence.[23]

The Ladies National Association presented the government with a petition signed by more than sixty-one thousand women, and another signed by seventy-three women doctors.[24] From the other side of the Atlantic came more criticism and condemnation. Lady Henry was accused of allying herself with vice and wickedness. For Bushnell and Andrew, who had risked their lives, suffered excessive heat and cold, and traveled thousands of

21 George W. Johnson and Lucy A. Johnson, eds., *Josephine E. Butler: An Autobiographical Memoir* (Bristol: J. W. Arrowsmith Ltd., 1909; reprint, 1928), 158.
22 Petrie, *Singular Iniquity*, 270.
23 Ibid.
24 Johnson and Johnson, eds., *Josephine E. Butler*, 176.

miles by water and rail to end these injustices to women, Lady Henry's action was blatant betrayal of all to which they had dedicated their lives. In a broadside sent to temperance organizations in both Britain and the United States, Bushnell and Andrew, shocked and enraged by this about-face, wrote:

> We believe that a crisis has come in the history of the W.C.T.U., and that God is weighing the organization in the balance. A great conflict of moral principles and in behalf of womanhood is being waged the world over, and God has himself sounded his battle cry. . . . Many have paused to question whether a retreat is possible, and God is waiting to see what the foremost organization of women in the world is willing to do in behalf of their own sex. England has sowed the wind by her cruel wrongs against India and other Oriental women in legalizing prostitution on the demand of profligate men, and England now fears the whirlwind.[25]

They also expressed doubts as to Lady Henry's commitment to absolute universal abstinence from alcohol and the use of tobacco by children. Bushnell, Andrew, and others less adamant prophesied that unless Lady Henry rescinded her endorsement of the acts, her influence in the American and World WCTA would be destroyed, and she would lose her position in the World organization.

Bushnell appealed to Willard as the one who had influence over Lady Henry, but to no avail. Although Willard felt that Lady Henry's actions were ill-advised, she expressed her view that the actions of the British in Britain were none of America's business. She insisted that the Women's Christian Temperance Union was concerned primarily with temperance, and that misguided though Lady Henry's actions might be, her purpose was sincere.[26]

In a letter to Willard, Lady Henry held fast: "Whether I am right or wrong I mean to keep the silence which 'answered never

---

25 *Chicago Tribune*, "A Crisis in the W.C.T.U."; *The Union Signal* 23 (18 November 1897), 3 (WCTU microfilm edition), roll 12, frame 097.

26 Ibid.; Fitzpatrick, *Lady Henry Somerset*, 202.

a word.' That is the one strength. I have said my say, time is my judge, time will prove if I am right, and I am content."[27]

Bushnell and Andrew were not so content. They saw their work of years undone by a word. To intensify the injury, their source of support and encouragement had turned on them. Incensed at this defense of Lady Henry, Bushnell wrote to Willard:

> . . . I am praying daily, hourly, and Mrs. [Andrew] is praying too concerning Lady Henry Somerset . . . I know God and I know He has heard and will hear our prayers, and that now the time is not long when that miserable woman's public career will be ended. . . . Possibly you may think if you could see us you could explain Lady Henry's position. You have no possible and creditable way of explaining why her praises are on the lips of every libertine and advocate of vice from Lord Roberts down. . . .
>
> And you are silent; even after appeal you are silent. And do you think God holds you guiltless for this silence? Do you think the American women will hold you guiltless? I know they will not. . . . May God pity you. I do. You have a heart and you have a conscience and in these regards you are perhaps less fortunate than Lady Henry Somerset, since you have chosen to let your vote go with hers by this silence. . . .
>
> Oh, that you had never met that woman of fatal fascination, to whom you swore that nothing would separate you from her, in either this world or the world to come, and nothing has separated you, as far as it appears—not even infamy as yet.[28]

Bushnell's words were strong and many considered them excessive. It was very difficult for her contemporaries and peers to understand Bushnell's apparent inability even to consider a viewpoint different from her own on this subject, or to comprehend the vehemence of her reaction to Lady Henry's reversal.

---

27 Fitzpatrick, *Lady Henry Somerset*, 201.
28 Ibid., 202–3. Lady Henry Somerset's biographer and literary executor did not name Bushnell or Andrew in this letter. However, she describes their visit to Reigate and the part Lady Henry had played in their earlier efforts. She refers to the two as "fanatic," as "virulent . . . American 'Uplifters,'" and is very uncomplimentary to them in other ways (pp. 201–4).

However, Bushnell had seen the terrible results of regulation at first hand, and had wept with the women who had experienced the degradation of government-sponsored prostitution. She could only view Lady Henry's suggestions as recommendations for legalized surgical rape and government support of immorality. The validity of her lifework was being called into question, and for Bushnell, reasonable reactions were not possible. Unfortunately for Bushnell's purpose, the passion of her attack, while it expressed the feelings of many, also aroused sympathy for Lady Henry and her views.

Contrary to the expectations of Lady Henry's detractors, she was re-elected as vice president of the World WCTU at the October annual convention in Toronto, Canada. When Bushnell and Andrew again protested, Willard, in her annual address to the WCTU in Buffalo, New York, once more supported Lady Henry's election and defended her conduct in supporting the modified Contagious Diseases Acts, although she also repeated her regrets at Lady Henry's actions. In the same address, she reprimanded Bushnell and Andrew, saying that they had "not a woman to stand by them and help them and go with them and preside at their meetings like Lady Henry Somerset. . . . I think that bitter denunciation of any co-worker implies a condition of heart that is not sweet toward God."[29]

The breach widened. On 19 November 1897 Josephine Butler, superintendent of the purity department of the World WCTU and mentor of Bushnell and Andrew, resigned her position "on account of the 'wavering or undecided' position of the leaders in reference to Regulation."[30] Other officials of that organization followed suit. Various WCTU branches around the world passed votes of censure.[31]

Of greater concern to Lady Henry was that the vituperative exchanges from both sides were affecting the health of Frances Willard. This, and the fact that there were no visible signs that the measures suggested in her letter were being implemented,

---

29 *The Union Signal* 23 (18 November 1897), 3–4 (WCTU microfilm edition), roll 12, frames 097, 098.

30 Wilson, *Rough Record*, no. 940.

31 Toronto *Mail-Empire*, 31 December 1897. From Willard Scrapbook.

caused Lady Henry to have second thoughts. On 7 February 1898, in a letter to Lord George Hamilton, Lady Henry Somerset once again reversed her position.

> Your Lordship invited me ten months ago to give you my view . . . and in a letter in which I did so I ventured to suggest some methods moral and disciplinary. . . . [I]n that time, nothing has been done of which the public has heard, to strengthen the forces that make for moral improvement. What has been done—viz., the repeal of the Indian Acts of 1895, which prohibited inspection, has been in a direction exactly opposite. . . . I find that my letter to your Lordship of last year has been taken by many to mean that I am on the side of the accepted view of State regulation, and I am from time to time quoted as a sympathizer with such views. I am therefore writing to withdraw any proposals made in that letter. . . .[32]

The retraction was greeted with joy by Willard, who was hoping that now the attacks against Lady Henry would stop, and she would be able to turn over the presidency of the World WCTU to her. But before she could see this happen, Willard died on 18 February 1898.[33] On the same day, Sir James Stanfeld, ardent supporter of Bushnell, Andrew, and Butler, also died.[34]

While many of the branches of the WCTU supported Lady Henry, opposition continued, and later in the spring of 1898 her position as president of the British Women's Temperance Association was once more challenged. At the association's annual public meeting in London on 10 May 1898, she again tendered her resignation, but the members again supported her and her reelection was met with a spontaneous ovation. She retained her position until 1903.[35]

---

32   *Woman's Signal,* 17 February 1898; *Chicago Daily Tribune,* 8 February 1898; *Chicago Post,* 8 February 1898. From Willard Scrapbook.

33   Fitzpatrick, *Lady Henry Somerset,* 207.

34   Wilson, *Rough Record,* nos. 958, 958a. Dates for these deaths are 17 February in *Rough Record,* possibly because Willard and Stansfeld died during the night of the 17th. Other reports give the 18th.

35   Ibid., 209–11. In 1903 Lady Henry Somerset retired from public life: initially to a settlement house for alcoholics in the East End of

In June, Mrs. Leavitt, honorary life president of the World WCTU, wrote an attack against Lady Henry Somerset and her views on temperance as well as social purity. Leavett was sure that the rank and file of the organization would rise up in protest. However, whatever the membership may have felt, those in leadership positions continued to support Lady Henry. Leavitt was criticized by the WCTU for "trying to judge one nation by the standards of another, and in assuming that what is deemed the best method of work among one people is necessarily best for all."[36] At the next annual convention of the World WCTU, in spite of all the opposition could do, Lady Henry Somerset was elected president and held that position until 1906.[37]

In a long and angry letter, written in London on 28 June 1898, and published in *The Union Signal* the following August, Andrew and Bushnell ended their long and productive relationship with the Women's Christian Temperance Union.[38] The letter concluded:

> For our own part, we believe we have immortal souls that will be saved or lost, according to whether or not we uphold the same moral standards the world over, without regard to custom or rank; without regard to whether the multitude is with us, or we "walk alone with God in the dark."
>
> Today we send our withdrawal of local membership in the W.C.T.U. Henceforth we are clear from the blood of all those who, in the organization, make compromise with iniquity. Heretofore, we have felt it a duty to sound the trumpet and warn of the approach of the enemy, as God commands the watchman

London, and finally at Duxhurst, a colony for inebriate women she had founded in 1895, located near her Reigate estate.

36 *The Union Signal* 24 (2 June 1898), 8–9 (WCTU microfilm edition), roll 12, frame 342.

37 Fitzpatrick, *Lady Henry Somerset,* 209.

38 Though we found no source giving the date of Andrew's and Bushnell's resignation from the World WCTU, we assume that it was at the same time Butler resigned. In any case, there was no further mention of them in *The Union Signal* or any other WCTU publication that we could locate.

to do in Ezekiel 33:1–9. That task is over, for the banner of
"expediency" is now held aloft, and the leaders of the W.C.T.U.
call on the rank and file to follow. The enemy is here. On each
one individually now rests the responsibility to act. We go our
way, a widely divergent one from that of the leaders of the
W.C.T.U. But be it known that like the house of David, the sword
will not soon depart from the W.C.T.U. for the folly that hath
this day been wrought in Israel.[39]

Andrew and Bushnell remained under Josephine Butler's
guidance during the rest of their stay in England, and the time
came when Butler sent for them and told them their mission in
social purity in England was finished. She told Bushnell that she
had "a message from God" for their future.[40] When they met,
Butler recommended that Bushnell turn her attention from social
purity work and toward holding meetings based on her Bible
studies.

Bushnell was elated. The social purity addresses had been
wearing on her nerves, and she had long been preparing for the
work of biblical interpretation. After discussion and prayer about
their plan of action, the three women agreed that "the social evil
would never be got rid of as long as the subordination of woman
to man was taught within the body of Christians." The crusade
for purity could never be completely successful until men and
women began to see that people of both sexes were of equal
value, and this would have to be proven by reinterpreting the
very passages that had always been used to subordinate women.

But place Christian women where God intends them to stand,
on a plane of full equality with men, in the home and in the
Church, where their faculties, their will, their consciences are
controlled only by the God who made man and woman equal
by creation, and who is "no respecter of persons"—then the
world will become much purer than it is today . . .[41]

---

39 *The Union Signal* 24 (4 August 1898), 6 (WCTU microfilm edition),
     roll 12, frame 402.
40 Bushnell, *Brief Sketch*, 22.
41 Ibid., 23, 24–25; the longer quote is from pp. 24–25.

Bushnell's long years of study of the Bible and biblical languages and her experience of working for justice for women were now to be carried out in that body of Christians. Shortly after this meeting with Butler, Andrew and Bushnell returned home, and Katharine Bushnell began her new work.

CHAPTER 6

SAN FRANCISCO
AND "SOCIAL HYGIENE"

ॐ

A fter her return from England, Bushnell became actively involved in Bible work[1] and writing. However, this work did not
preclude her continuing to seek out social injustice, particularly
that involving the degradation of women. Following their homecoming, she and Elizabeth Andrew engaged in writing a history
of "yellow" slavery in Hong Kong and China, later published as
Heathen Slaves and Christian Rulers, and this led them to the
investigation of the related traffic in prostitution in the United
States, particularly in San Francisco's Chinatown. In Hong Kong
they had found evidence of the trade between China and San
Francisco brothel proprietors, and they followed this evidence
into San Francisco itself.[2]

Bushnell had settled in Oakland, California, in 1904,[3] and
evidence of forced prostitution existed close by. Prior to the great

---

1 While Bushnell says that she is doing Bible "work" (*Brief Sketch,*
  26), she never tells us exactly what the "work" is: whether teaching,
  research, study, writing, or all of these. We know she wrote and
  circulated the Bible correspondence course, but we do not know
  the details of how this was organized.
2 We have found no date for the final return of Bushnell and Andrew
  from the round-the-world tours. We know only that Bushnell settled
  in Oakland in 1904, and that *Heathen Slaves and Christian Rulers* was
  written in 1907. We assume that the investigations of the China-San
  Francisco slave trade occurred during this period.
3 Hoppin, "Legacy of Katharine Bushnell."

San Francisco earthquake in April 1906, the Chinese and Japanese brothels were restricted to San Francisco; after the destruction in that disaster, a huge brothel with an estimated population varying from 150 to 300 could be found in Oakland also. At the time of Bushnell's inspection of the building, it housed 125 Japanese and 50 Chinese women, and another 100 Chinese women were expected within days.[4]

This large house of prostitution in Oakland was owned by Americans and managed by a European,[5] and "watch-dogs" who guarded the women were also Caucasians. The Chinese traders preferred not to have direct contact with the Caucasian women working in the rescue missions, and the primary function of the "watch-dogs" was to "prevent the entrance of mission workers to rescue slaves."[6] Andrew and Bushnell uncovered the same kinds of complicity on the part of law enforcement agencies that they had found in India, China, and Hong Kong.[7] Caucasian lawyers defended those engaging in the slave trade and were frequently able to accomplish the return of young women who had been rescued by the missions. Using writs of *habeus corpus* and false accusations such as stealing against the prostitutes, these lawyers were able to have guardianship of prostitutes taken away from the missions and returned to the prostitutes' former owners.

Bushnell and Andrew attributed this trade largely to the participation of European and American Caucasian males.[8] Stringent laws against the slave trade made participation in it lucra-

---

4 Andrew and Bushnell, *Heathen Slaves and Christian Rulers*, 146, 147.

5 Ibid., 147.

6 Ibid., 141. The Chinese proprietors or "pocket-mothers" (owners of individual prostitutes in a larger brothel) were fearful of "arousing race-prejudice" if they guarded their own slaves from the Caucasian missionaries who made daring forays into the brothels for rescue purposes (141–42).

7 Ibid., 142.

8 Bushnell claims that these slave pens and slave brothels were "practically unknown in the regions of China uninfluenced by Western civilization." Andrew and Bushnell, *Heathen Slaves and Christian Rulers*, 141.

tive for those willing to take the risk: the market price for a new young woman from China was three thousand dollars at the time Andrew and Bushnell undertook their investigations.[9] One of the most common procedures for bringing Chinese women into this country for illicit purposes was for the agent to go to China, purchase and marry the woman, and bring her to the United States. On the voyage, the "wife" would be indoctrinated as to her new life and would be filled with great fear of the consequences of trying to escape or to send to the rescue missions in San Francisco for help. She was told that the missionaries would starve her and beat her daily if she sought refuge in the missions,[10] and few women dared to appeal for help either to the authorities or to the missions.

The situation in San Francisco was exacerbated by the habit within well-to-do Chinese families of keeping one or more household slaves. These slaves could, at the will of the owner, be sold to brothels or taken as concubines. Children born to prostitutes and household slaves were considered to be the property of the slave's owner and could, like their mothers, be sold outright. The girls were introduced to prostitution around the age of fifteen, and there were celebrations at the initiation of a virgin into the life of prostitution, a special price being paid by Caucasian males for the privilege of the initial rape.[11] The baby boys were frequently sold to Chinese men as adopted sons; the legal wives and sons of the men remained in China, so the husbands would purchase prostitutes from the brothels as concubines and second wives. As they would have no children by the concubine, they would purchase and adopt sons.[12] Polygamy was practiced,

---

9 Ibid., 145.

10 One case was cited in which a young refugee escaped from a brothel and entered into one of the missions. On her first night in the mission, she waited up long after her fellows had retired, and when she was asked why, she replied that she was waiting for her beating. Ibid., 148.

11 Andrew and Bushnell, *Heathen Slaves and Christian Rulers,* 140–41. According to Bushnell, Chinese men would not take part in this "deflowering," either "through moral sense or superstition" (141).

12 We are not told why the Chinese men would not have children by

since the "admixture of the brothel element with all Chinese home life in the United States [made] this country very undesirable as a residence for virtuous Chinese women."[13]

While they made some of their inquiries in person, Bushnell and Andrew were not active to the extent that they had been in their crusades in India, China, or Hong Kong. They relied in large part on public documents and on research into the records of the Presbyterian and Methodist Mission Rescue Homes of San Francisco.[14]

Within a few years after the publication of *Heathen Slaves and Christian Rulers*, Bushnell returned to England to study biblical literature and languages at the great university libraries available to her there. While engaged in her studies, Bushnell wrote the lessons for her Bible correspondence course that were eventually to be gathered into her principal work, *God's Word to Women*.[15] After seven years of this study and writing, Bushnell returned to America.[16] She conducted her correspondence course for several years, issuing the mimeographed lessons periodically.[17]

With the U.S. involvement in the First World War came the inauguration of a "Federal Social Hygiene programme"[18] that

---

the prostitutes they had purchased, or why purchasing baby boys born to prostitutes was more desirable than fathering one's own child.

13 Andrew and Bushnell, *Heathen Slaves and Christian Rulers*, 148.
14 Ibid., 151.
15 Bushnell, *Brief Sketch*, 24.
16 We were able to find no information on the exact date or reason for her return. Events were transpiring which led up to the First World War, and these events may have encouraged her to come home. We know she spent seven years after Butler's death (1906) in England. We also know she published a final edition of one of her works in England in 1914 and an edition of *The Women's Correspondence Bible Class* in 1916, so we assume she returned between 1914 and 1916.
17 Penn-Lewis, *"Magna Charta" of Woman*, 13.
18 Katharine Bushnell, "What's Going On: a report of investigations by Katharine C. Bushnell, regarding certain social and legal abuses in

Katharine Bushnell considered to be a plan for "healthy vice for our soldiers, and that through the destruction of the constitutional rights of women."[19] This program involved the "surgical rape"[20] of any woman or girl suspected of having, or reported to have, venereal disease. This issue, of course, was the one Bushnell had battled for a great part of her life, both in her journey to India for Josephine Butler and in her inquiries in Hong Kong and China for the British government. California cities were declared by Washington to be "a 'model' for all the other states,"[21] and to see government-supported "regulation of vice" begin in her own country, her own back yard, was an issue that drew her away from her Bible studies in an effort to expose and eliminate the abuses.

Once again, as she had in Wisconsin, in India, and in Hong Kong, Bushnell went into the red-light districts, visited hospitals, and interviewed doctors. The report she issued under the title "What's Going On"[22] reflects her anger at the injustice and the indignity suffered by women. To the argument that one woman could infect twenty men in a night, she replied that in that case "there are about twenty men to one woman practicing vice; and the thing resolves itself into the simple arithmetical rule that, if one woman may do the mischief of twenty men, then twenty men may do the mischief of one woman."[23]

To Bushnell, there was no measuring the difference between the reward or punishment meted out to men or to women. The men received "early" or "prophylactic" treatment, whether or not they knew the woman with whom they had sexual relations was "diseased." As Bushnell wrote in her report, "this is treatment

---

California that have been in part aggravated and in part created by the Federal Social Hygiene programme" (Oakland, CA: By the author, 1919), 1.

19 Bushnell, *Brief Sketch*, 26.
20 A phrase used frequently by Bushnell in this report and in her report of her work in India. She refers to the forcible examination of women to determine whether they were carriers of venereal disease.
21 Bushnell, "What's Going On," 1.
22 We do not know to whom this report was issued.
23 Bushnell, "What's Going On," 2.

primarily of the fornication or adultery, as the case may be."
Simple suspicion, however, was enough to require a woman to
be examined and quarantined. Further, since prostitutes were
automatically classed as vagrants, the health officers assumed
that all female vagrants were prostitutes. They acted accordingly
and forced women charged with vagrancy to submit to examination and to quarantine.[24] To make matters worse, all a soldier or
a sailor had to do was to report any woman as suspicious, or as
the source of his disease, and that woman would be picked up,
detained in a hospital, and examined.[25]

Bushnell deplored the blatant injustice to women manifested
in the unequal amounts of shame and punishment suffered by
equal partners to the immorality. Never did she condone the
immoral behavior of either party to the illicit sex act. Her desire
was for justice for both parties: the same punishment, the same
shame meted out for both the man and the woman involved. She
was incensed that the men would always go free, while the
women lost all rights, including that of *habeus corpus* and due
process of law. Under the terms and instructions of the federal
hygiene program, women were to be held and their trials post-
poned so they could be examined and treated if necessary. The
men were to be tried and sentenced immediately. "Men are to
have their constitutional rights respected, even to being free to
infect their innocent wives and children!"[26]

Bushnell roundly condemned this program as promoting
"guilty, vicious practices"[27] on the part of servicemen. As in India,
she tried to show that regulation did not stop vice, but promoted
it. Once again she traveled—investigating, giving speeches, ex-
horting—but this time to no avail. She sent pamphlets and letters
to the president of the United States, his cabinet, the Senate, and
the House of Representatives. Although she was supported in

---

24   Ibid., 2, 4.
25   Bushnell cites many cases in which "decent" women were detained.
     Some did submit to examination just to regain their freedom; others
     refused to submit and instituted lawsuits. Bushnell, "What's Going
     On," 6–9, etc.
26   Ibid., 12.
27   Ibid., 14.

her crusade by the contributions of a few who concurred with her views, she found no widespread sympathy or cooperation. She felt her campaign for decency was "completely beaten,"[28] and in the end, the great effort expended in this most bitter of all her crusades was in vain.

Bushnell resumed her Bible study and her writing. During these years she was supported in part by her nephew, William Bushnell Stout, a writer and an inventor.[29] In the late 1920s Bushnell decided to return to China to offer more help to the people she had loved and served throughout her life, although she felt that at her age there was little she could do.[30] She went to Shanghai, where she remained for a few years, working in the pediatric hospital she had established.[31] The invasion of Manchurian China by the Japanese in 1931 forced her to return to her home in California.[32]

In an article that appeared in *The Christian Advocate* in 1942, four years before Bushnell's death, her pastor described her life at that time:

> Today, at an age when most people would be content with their memories, Dr. Bushnell is continually at work. She maintains a large world-wide correspondence, and within the last few

---

28 Bushnell, *Brief Sketch,* 27.
29 *The National Union Catalog Pre-1956 Imprints,* vol. 87 (London: Mansell Information/Publishing Ltd., 1970), shows five books on flying, mechanical models, etc. Stout was also the designer of the Kaiser-Frazer automobile ("Bushnell Services Conducted," San Francisco *Post Enquirer,* 28 January 1946), photocopy from manager of Truman's Funeral Directors. Bushnell's will instructs that "whatever money may still be left, to be returned from whence it came- [sic] to William Bushnell Stout." Bushnell's "Last Will and Testament."
30 Bushnell, *Brief Sketch,* 28.
31 "Bushnell Rites Set for Monday," *Oakland Tribune,* 27 January 1946. Copy of article sent by Truman's Funeral Directors to Ruth Hoppin in Daly City, California. A letter from the manager of the funeral home says this article was in the Oakland paper.
32 Bushnell, *Brief Sketch,* 28 [editorial note].

months has finished the manuscript of a new book. There is no such word as "retired" in the vocabulary of this Methodist crusader.[33]

Katharine C. Bushnell died on Friday, 25 January 1946,[34] ten days short of her ninety-first birthday, leaving behind a treasure of Bible studies of which little use has been made. As her last pastor, Dr. K. Fillmore Gray, remarked, "Her work was like a rock dropped to the bottom of the ocean. Kerplunk, it was gone, the end of it."[35]

---

33 K. Fillmore Gray, "Crusader," *The Christian Advocate*, 8 January 1942. (From typed copy of the article received from Dr. Bushnell's great-niece.) We have been able to find no record of the contents or publication of the book manuscript mentioned by Gray, although Bushnell published a number of pamphlets between 1938 and 1945.
34 "Bushnell Rites Set"; "Bushnell Services Conducted." Both of these obituaries give the day of death as Friday, which would be 25 January 1946, not 26 January. Hoppin, "Legacy of Katharine Bushnell," 6, gives the date as 26 January 1946.
35 Hoppin, "Legacy of Katharine Bushnell," 6.

CHAPTER 7

THE LAST CRUSADE: THE WRITINGS

❧

B ushnell's final crusade was waged on paper and was the culmination and justification of a life spent in the service of God and of humanity. Her call to service was tested and redirected through the failure of her health early in her medical missionary work in China, and her long journey in answer to that new call began. She saw women's need universally because she traveled the world over and was witness to the abuse of women everywhere she went. Each major crusade she undertook added to her conviction of the need to have the power of the Bible behind woman's search for freedom; each mile journeyed on each crusade increased the motivation for her journey into the Bible.

In China, Bushnell began to see how biblical translation could influence and promote the degradation and the suppression of women. When she answered the call to turn from medicine to evangelism, she found the same suffering among women in the streets of Chicago. In her forays against prostitution in Wisconsin lumber camps, Bushnell faced the reality of the investment both men and "virtuous" women had in continuing a system that degraded women. Her crusades in Wisconsin, India, Hong Kong, and China, and her experiences battling Parliament in England, convinced her of government's complicity in the support and regulation of vice; this complicity showed her how deeply the institutionalization of vice was ingrained in "civilized" society.

Bushnell faced opposition again and again, not only from those who reaped their fortunes from prostitution, but also from some of the prostitutes themselves, and she found the reason for this in women's traditional lack of freedom. In the fictionalized version of her biblical interpretations, *The Reverend Doctor and His Doctor Daughter,* Bushnell admits to bitterness and speaks with anger on the subject of the freedom of women.[1] When the "Reverend" accuses his daughter of speaking bitterly, she replies:

> I speak as I feel. Men have taken upon themselves the task of governing, managing, and tutoring women, almost throughout the world's history. It was to be supposed that men would have modestly stood on one side and let Christ take the matter in hand, after woman alone [in human terms] brought Christ into the world,—but no, even since then they must continue to hold the reins of government over women, just as they did when pagans. Do they not understand that *there can be no morality for women apart from freedom?* They understand this with their *sons,* and soon put them, as they advance towards manhood, on an increasingly independent footing, that the youths may develop strength of character; but their [women] must be under perpetual management or tutelage from their birth to the grave; with no free choice between right and wrong, no free will apart from interference.

Reminded of the increasing freedom of women, the "daughter" replies that this is only in America and England; Bushnell saw the need for freedom to be universal. Further, this freedom had not been accomplished through the church as it should have been.[2] And as the church was not freeing women to be all they could be, Bushnell turned to the Bible and biblical commentaries to determine why.

Bushnell first became interested in Bible study during her years as a medical missionary in China. While reading a Chinese

---

1 Jessie Penn-Lewis says that "nothing but the grace of God has enabled [Bushnell] to write so temperately" given the things she had done and seen during her crusades. Penn-Lewis, *"Magna Charta" of Woman,* 16–17.

2 Katharine Bushnell, *The Reverend Doctor and His Doctor Daughter* (Oakland, CA: By the author, 1927), 54, 55. The quotation is on p. 54.

translation, she noticed that the word "woman" was left out of Philippians 4:3, "I entreat thee, also, true yoke-fellow, help those women which labored. . . ." This translation replaces "woman" with "true yoke-fellows."[3] Upon investigation, she found that three other Chinese translations did the same. She began making other comparisons between her Greek New Testament and the Chinese translations and discovered that the Chinese translations had been deliberately biased because of "pagan prejudice against the ministry of women."[4] The longer she worked in the mission field, the more convinced she became that the biased translations done by men were the source of the prejudice against women. The longer she worked for the equality of women, the more Bushnell realized that woman's plight was rooted in the fact that the Bible was seen to support the degradation and suppression of women. Her conclusion was that the Bible needed to be reinterpreted, and her task was to develop an interpretation that would free women to seek their "proper place in the divine economy."[5]

Bushnell saw divine guidance in the integration of study and service that informed her writing. In looking back over her life, Bushnell notes that

> it was according to a Divine plan that the . . . investigations in the Orient should have gone forward hand in hand, as it were, with my Bible studies—for nearly every moment of my many sea voyages and railway journeys was spent in these studies. (Fortunately my early training in a home crowded with nine children and little privacy had developed powers of detachment from surroundings, allowing mental concentration.)[6]

Given a life spent in active lecture and on mission fields, to turn to writing and Bible study meant a major refocusing of Bushnell's efforts and a new understanding of her call to ministry. This step was taken neither lightly nor without interference.

---

3 Frances E. Willard, *Woman in the Pulpit* (Boston: D. Lothrup Company, 1888), 31.

4 Bushnell, *Brief Sketch,* 20; Willard, *Woman in the Pulpit,* 32.

5 From the full title of *God's Word to Women.*

6 Bushnell, *Brief Sketch,* 20.

When Butler called Bushnell and Andrew back to London and told them it was time to change their focus, she encouraged Bushnell to begin holding the kind of "general Christian meetings" for which her Bible studies and knowledge of the original biblical languages had well prepared her.[7] Bushnell reports, "I then opened my heart freely to Mrs. Butler, telling her how I had longed to give Bible instruction on the lines of purity, and to show the importance of the freedom of women for the purification of society; and how I had been, all along, preparing for such activity."[8] Butler gave her blessing to Bushnell's growing vision, and having thus been commissioned for her new crusade, Bushnell turned her attention to Bible study and writing.

Bushnell maintained that it was not possible to study and write about the Bible properly without an intimate knowledge of the biblical languages. She had begun the study of Latin and Greek in her classics course at Northwestern[9] in 1873. With this foundation she was competent enough, while in China, to compare her Chinese and Greek texts and to conclude that a strong and detrimental gender bias existed in the Chinese version.[10] Her interest was caught and she intensified her study, first of the Greek New Testament and then of the Septuagint. From there she proceeded to Hebrew, which she learned by independent study.[11] While she felt herself to be competent in Greek, she never had the same confidence in her Hebrew translations,[12] and corresponded regularly with professors who had greater expertise.[13]

---

7   Ibid., 23; Penn-Lewis, *"Magna Charta" of Woman*, 13.

8   Bushnell, *Brief Sketch*, 23.

9   Willard, "Bushnell, A Sketch"; Bushnell, *Reverend Doctor*, 7–8. This is a fictional work, but there are several biographical elements in it, and we feel that this is one of them.

10 Bushnell, *Brief Sketch*, 20.

11 Bushnell, *Reverend Doctor*, 9. Bushnell names the texts she used in her independent study: Harper's *Elements of Hebrew* and *Method and Manual*. Again, this is a fictional work, but it is also meant to be instructional, and Bushnell frequently notes texts that she uses as sources in her other works.

12 Bushnell, *Brief Sketch*, 20.

13 Bushnell, *God's Word to Women*, author's note. Bushnell's usual

By the time Bushnell returned to England (about 1907),[14] she was fairly well grounded in the biblical languages, but the purpose of her return at that time was to polish her language skills and to intensify her biblical study in the English university libraries. It was while engaged in these studies that she began to write a Bible correspondence course for women.

Bushnell's work falls into two categories: reports of her crusades[15] and Bible studies of varying lengths.[16] Bushnell began to publish her work regularly while she was in England, but she had published several other works during her career as a missionary and an evangelist. Other than the pamphlets and some articles in *The Union Signal,* Bushnell's first published work was *A Clean Life* (Women's Temperance Publishing Association, 1896). Bushnell and Elizabeth Andrew collaborated on the story of their crusade in India, *The Queen's Daughters in India,* publish-

---

correspondent was Dr. A. Mingana, Professor of Arabic at Manchester University, England, and Curator of Oriental Manuscripts in the John Rylands Library. Bushnell sent him her correspondence lessons, and is very conscientious about including his opinions, both pro and con, of her nontraditional interpretations.

14 A date of 1907 is an educated guess, based on the information in Hoppin, "Legacy of Katharine Bushnell," and the statement by Bushnell in *Brief Sketch* (20) that she returned after Butler's death (1906).

15 "Work in Northern Wisconsin" reports on Bushnell's efforts to stop forced prostitution in the Wisconsin lumber towns; *The Queen's Daughters in India* reports the Indian campaign against state-regulated prostitution in the British military installations in India; *Heathen Slaves and Christian Rulers* reports the investigations in Hong Kong and China of the opium trade and the trade in female slaves for the purposes of prostitution, and also reports the connected trade in Oriental women in San Francisco. "What's Going On?" reports Bushnell's futile crusade against the U.S. Army's "Social Hygiene" program.

16 Bushnell, *God's Word to Women.* Many of her other Bible study works are offshoots from this one. Studies not included in *God's Word to Women* are *The Vashti-Esther Bible Story* and *The Supreme Virtue* (Song of Solomon). See the annotated bibliography.

ed in England in 1898; and in 1907 they wrote *Heathen Slaves and Christian Rulers,* a similar report on forced prostitution in China, Hong Kong, and San Francisco.

After Bushnell's return to England, she began to publish her Bible studies in various forms. *God's Word to Women: 101 Questions Answered,* was first published in 1910, with new editions in 1912 and 1914.[17] This work was not the Bible studies that would also be called by the same main title. The first form of that work appeared in 1911 under the name *Woman's Correspondence Bible Class,* and the work was revised and expanded until the last edition, which appeared in 1930. Bushnell continued to publish other Bible studies and various spinoffs from *God's Word to Women* under her own aegis until 1945, the year before her death.[18]

In 1911, the first generation of the *Women's Correspondence Bible Class* appeared in London as a series of Bible lessons "reproduced from typewriting."[19] A second edition appeared in 1912, which was revised and reissued in 1913 as *God's Word to Women: The Women's Correspondence Bible Class.* It was still a series and it was still "reproduced from typewriting." After Bushnell returned to the United States, the forty-eight lessons were bound together and in 1916 were published by the author as the first American edition of *God's Word to Women.* This version was paperbound and was subtitled "Forty-eight Bible Lessons of the Women's Correspondence Bible Class." In 1922,[20] a clothbound

---

17   The editions and publication dates are reconstructed from *British Musuem General Catalogue of Printed Books to 1955,* vol. 4, the *National Union Catalog Pre-1956 Imprints,* vol. 87, and estimated from various annotated partial bibliographies in Bushnell's publications.

18   See the annotated bibliography for as complete a list as we have been able to compile.

19   *British Museum General Catalogue of Printed Books to 1955,* vol. 4, compact ed. (New York: Readex Microprint Corporation, 1967), 984. We do not know what kind of technology would "reproduce from typewriting" in 1911. Penn-Lewis, *"Magna Charta" of Woman,* 13, says she used a mimeograph.

20   Hoppin, "Legacy of Katharine Bushnell," 6. We have been unable to find any other date or evidence of this clothbound edition, and

edition of the book was published in two volumes of forty-eight lessons each, which Bushnell describes as the first edition.[21] In 1923, Bushnell expanded the book to one hundred lessons and this second (or third) edition was published with its final title: *God's Word to Women: One Hundred Bible Studies on Woman's Place in the Divine Economy.* The fourth and last edition was issued from China in 1930 with a new preface.[22]

God's Word to Women did not make much of a stir. In 1924 it was critically reviewed in *The Sunday School Times* by Griffith Thomas, who found much that was enlightening, but also some views that he felt were unwarranted. He warned against the author's "overeagerness to prove her case."[23] In the same year, Helen Barrett Montgomery gave the book only praise in her review, recommending it in "Good Books for Busy Pastors" for *The Baptist.*[24] At this point all mention of the book disappeared—"kerplunk, it was gone, the end of it"[25]—until it resurfaced nearly fifty years later.

Bushnell herself gives no dates.

21 Katharine C. Bushnell, *The Supreme Virtue: Loyalty to God's Anointed King* (Oakland, CA: Katharine C. Bushnell, 1924), 58. This back page describes this first edition as having ninety-six lessons in two volumes, and suggests that "now is the time for those who have bought only Volume One to complete the set." Since the only previous "volume" was that of forty-eight lessons, we are assuming that this second volume also contains forty-eight lessons.

22 Katharine C. Bushnell, "Introduction to the Fourth Edition," *God's Word to Women.* It is possible that the third edition was published in England, as a third edition is listed in an annotated bibliography in *Brief Sketch,* which was published in England.

23 Griffith Thomas, review of *God's Word to Women* by Katharine C. Bushnell, in *The Sunday School Times,* 22 March 1924, 200.

24 Helen Barrett Montgomery, review of *God's Word to Women* by Katharine C. Bushnell, in "Good Books for Busy Pastors," *The Baptist* S (1924–25): 557–58. The book was also mentioned favorably in *The Christian* (London), 15 May 1924, and *The Australian Biblical Recorder* (April 1924). Noted in Katharine C. Bushnell, *Mother's Catechism on Adam and Eve* (Oakland, CA: By the author, 1938).

25 Gray, "Crusader."

In the mid-1950s, while preaching at a revival on an Indian reservation, a part-time Pentecostal preacher was given a copy of an out-of-print booklet, *The "Magna Charta" of Woman According to the Scriptures* by Jessie Penn-Lewis,[26] a work that was based on Bushnell's book, *God's Word to Women*.[27] The preacher, Ray Munson, began a search for the work on which the *"Magna Charta" of Woman* had been based, a search that resulted in the reprinting of *God's Word to Women* in the mid-1970s.[28]

The book's other publishers, Bernice Menold and Cosette Joliff of Peoria, Illinois, also were exposed to Bushnell's work through Penn-Lewis's *Magna Charta*. They began a search for the original, but were unsuccessful. Finally, Menold wrote the Library of Congress and purchased the layout from the library for eighty-five dollars. Finding the book fascinating and full of new insights about women and their role in the church, Menold and Joliff decided to investigate the possibility of reprinting. They met someone who knew of Munson's connection with the book, and after contacting him, agreed to take over publication.[29] The book is still in print, largely because these publishers believe that it has an important contribution to make. Bushnell's 1923 edition of *God's Word to Women* was the version finally found by Munson and is the reprint being circulated today.[30]

Although it is cited in one major commentary, *God's Word to Women* has, for the most part, been ignored by critical scholars. And yet, at least one of Bushnell's insights is currently being promoted as a "new" discovery in New Testament exegesis.[31]

---

26 Penn-Lewis, *"Magna Charta" of Woman.*
27 Hearn, "New Publishers of Katharine Bushnell," 5–6.
28 Ibid., 6.
29 From a copy of an article appearing in *West Bluff Word* sent by Menold and Joliff. *God's Word to Women* is available from two sources; see the annotated bibliography.
30 There was a fourth version, put together in Shanghai. Bushnell's will mentions the "'shells' (made in Shanghai) for a fourth edition of 'God's Word to Women' [sic]." This edition was printed.
31 Dowd, "Old Roots," 2–3.

CHAPTER 8

BUSHNELL
AND THE BIBLE

꿍

T he reinterpretation of several key passages in Genesis is crucial to Bushnell's arguments in the whole of *God's Word to Women*. She feels the early chapters of Genesis are a valuable history for women, but finds a number of interpretations that have caused women great suffering. A number of contemporary scholars agree with this view: "it has been argued, for example, that the roots of condoning wife battery can be found in the Old Testament account of Eve's sin and her subsequent punishment, a story which helped make women culturally legitimate objects of antagonism."[1] In *God's Word to Women*, Bushnell carefully analyzes such debatable interpretations, citing the authorities of her day, giving her own judgments, and then stating and defending her own position. She corresponded regularly with Hebrew scholars, and presents their opinions, both positive and negative, in footnotes throughout *God's Word to Women*.

Genesis 1:26–28

Bushnell begins her exegesis of passages of particular interest to women with Genesis 1:26–28: "Let us make man in our image, after our likeness. . . . So God created man in his own image, in the image of God he created him; male and female he created them." She highlights the point that the blessings of

---

1 Nehama Aschkenasy, *Eve's Journey: Feminine Images in Hebraic Literary Tradition* (Philadelphia: University of Pennsylvania Press, 1986), 9.

Genesis 1:28 are pronounced to both male and female—that with God "we observe the perfect equality of the sexes."[2]

This view is supported and further elaborated in many modern treatments. Citing Bushnell throughout his own work, Maxwell sees "[m]ale and female oneness . . . clearly set forth . . . equal in all essential respects. . . ."[3] Jewett says, "Since men and women are equally in the image of God, what is true for one is true for the other," and further, this implies a partnership with God in life.[4] Sexual differentiation, maintains Trible, designates equality and not a subordinate/superior hierarchy.[5] Creation, blessing, and granting of dominion all imply both equality and harmony, suggests Tischler: "a happy balance of opposites that compose the whole of [humanity]."[6] Evans finds full humanity "not in the male alone, but in man and woman," and "no hint of subordination of one sex to the other . . . no distinction between male and female in their creation as in the image of God or as in having dominion over all the earth."[7] With this view Mickelsen agrees and sees male and female given identical and equal responsibility and dominion over creation. She also finds "Adam" as humankind belonging equally to male and female, a concept with which Bushnell would agree. Bushnell and Mickelsen are also parallel in seeing the five blessings for men and women and that responsibility for the world is shared. Mickelsen notes Bushnell as one of several biblical scholars refuting the "traditional way of seeing male dominance as part of the divine plan."[8]

---

2 Bushnell, *God's Word to Women,* par. 25.

3 L. E. Maxwell, *Women in Ministry* (Wheaton: Victor, 1987), 36.

4 Paul K. Jewett, *Man as Male and Female* (Grand Rapids: Eerdmans, 1975), 131, 13–14.

5 Phyllis Trible, *God and the Rhetoric of Sexuality* (Philadelphia: Fortress, 1978), 18.

6 Nancy M. Tischler, *Legacy of Eve: Women of the Bible* (Atlanta: John Knox, 1977), 15.

7 Mary J. Evans, *Woman in the Bible: An Overview of All the Crucial Passages on Women's Roles* (Downers Grove: InterVarsity, 1983), 12.

8 Alvera Mickelson, "An Egalitarian View: There Is Neither Male Nor Female in Christ," in *Women in Ministry: Four Views,* Bonnidell Clouse and Robert G. Clouse, eds. (Downers Grove: InterVarsity,

Hull sees equality of the sexes in humanity, and redemption necessary to any possibility of change.[9] Although Foh does assert that the woman "is functionally subordinate to her husband," she agrees with the concept of of "equality in being" and says that "there is nothing in the text to suggest any difference between them. Both man and woman are equally in the image of God . . . have the same relationship to God (in his image) and to nature (to fill and exercise dominion over)."[10]

Genesis 2:18–22

Bushnell's next assertions are less universally held. She understands Genesis 2:18, "It is not good that the man should be alone," to mean that Adam was alone because he had become separated from God prior to Eve's formation. Bushnell cites support for her interpretation from William Law, Alexander White, and Jacob Boehme. Before Eve was "taken out," Adam turned his attention and desire (whether sensual or not) toward the lower animals and away from God. Eve's creation as helper was to lead Adam out of this fallenness. Bushnell understands the purpose of the division as being the "INDEPENDENCE OF THE FEMALE from all dominion but God's." Further, she sees any attempt to "submerge [Eve's] identity in man" to be a frustration of, and contrary to, God's plan.[11]

Having established this to her satisfaction, Bushnell turns her attention to what she terms "The Fable of the Rib," contending that this is a "stupid mistranslation" of the Hebrew word meaning "side," "chamber," or "corner." This word is never translated as "rib" anywhere in the Bible except in Genesis 2:21–22. Her conclusion is that Eve was built from one of Adam's sides, "or one part of Adam's being," the female part. She says "God

---

1989), 173–206.

9 Gretchen Gaebelein Hull, *Equal to Serve: Women and Men in the Church and Home* (Old Tappan, NJ: Revell, 1987), 194.

10 Susan T. Foh, "A Male Leadership View: The Head of the Woman Is the Man," in Clouse and Clouse, eds., *Women in Ministry*, 72–73.

11 Bushnell, *God's Word to Women*, par. 31, 32–33, 170. Emphasis Bushnell's.

took one of Adam's sides . . . out of which he 'builded' her."[12] Mickelsen, along the same lines, says, "God . . . took some of the man's own body and from it 'built' . . . the woman. . . . Adam recognized that Eve was 'made of the same stuff' as he and therefore should be the equal that God knew he needed to share the responsibility in the world."[13]

Bushnell goes so far as to posit the original Adam as androgynous[14] and cites rabbinic and scientific sources for support. Rambau, in his commentary on the Torah, supports this theory, citing Rabbi Yirmeyahu in positing two "faces," male and female, for the initial human. He further states that one face, the helper, was separated and "stands facing him, and that he should see and be separated from it or joint to it at his will."[15]

Genesis 3:16

Bushnell bases much of her theology on a corrected translation of Genesis 3:16b: "Yet your desire shall be for your husband, and he shall rule over you." She points out some of the logical consequences of viewing all women as living out Eve's curse: that marriage and husband are God's curses upon women; that the Talmudic Ten Curses, including man's right to be polygamous, are valid; that Adam was rewarded for his disobedience with license to rule and subordinate women to his lust;[16] that "man" is relieved of the necessity to keep the Decalogue, being able to commit adultery (which Bushnell maintains is anything other than strict monogamy); that the woman is to make her husband into an idol which she worships in place of God. Scripture explicitly says none of these things, but Bushnell sees them as implied and feels they illustrate the necessity for a retranslation of this passage that will not lead to these conclusions.

---

12 Ibid., par. 36, 40, 39 (Bushnell quotes Wilberforce on Eve having been fashioned from Adam's rib and elaborates), 43–44.

13 Mickelsen, "An Egalitarian View," in *Women in Ministry,* 183.

14 *God's Word to Women,* par. 24, 43.

15 Rambau, *Commentary on the Torah: Genesis* (New York: Shilo, 1971), 76.

16 Bushnell, *God's Word to Women,* par. 109, 106, 105.

Genesis 3:16 appears in the Authorized Version as "I will greatly multiply thy sorrow." Bushnell translated this as "a snare" or a "lying-in-wait [ie., the serpent] hath increased thy sorrow."[17] She based her translation on what she viewed as an erronous use of the Hebrew interlinear vowel-signs, which were not added until centuries after the original text had been written and which reflect the male bias. Bushnell submitted her translation to a "high authority in the Hebrew Language," who disagreed, finding it "unnatural or . . . unduly forced, where the usual rendering is natural."[18] Bushnell, of course, disagreed with his judgment, seeing this as one more example of male bias. She admitted in a later publication that she had been unable to find any support in ancient manuscripts for her position,[19] but she still held to it. Bushnell's contemporary, Lee Anna Starr, based her similar opinion on Bushnell, quoting the appropriate sections in her own work and arguing further from the Hebrew.[20]

Genesis 3:16b is of greater importance to the question of women's freedom from submission to men, and Bushnell translated this as "Thou art turning away [from God] to thy husband, and he will rule over thee." This translation, "turning away," is based on the Hebrew word *teshuqa*. Bushnell began her discussion by attacking the verb form "shall be," saying it is added by the translator, therefore making the desire imperative, and putting God's approval—nay, God's command!—on unbridled lust.[21] She says there is no third person imperative in Hebrew.[22] Trible supports this, rendering the passage "For your man is your desire, but he will rule over you."[23]

Next Bushnell takes the translation of the verb *teshuqa* to task. This word is translated "desire" or "appetite" in its occur-

17 Ibid., par. 117. Bushnell claims that the Septuagint and "many ancient authorities" support her in this interpretation (par. 121).

18 Ibid., par. 117; par. 119, citing an authority she does not name.

19 Bushnell, *Reverend Doctor,* 74.

20 Lee Anna Starr, *The Bible Status of Woman* (1926; Zarephath, NJ: Pillar of Fire, 1955), 43–44.

21 Bushnell, *God's Word to Women,* par. 124, 129.

22 Bushnell, *Reverend Doctor,* 74.

23 Trible, *God and the Rhetoric of Sexuality,* 127.

rences in the Authorized Version. Bushnell, however, finds "turning" a more accurate rendering based on the verb *shuq,* which means to run back and forth.[24] Her study of the church fathers shows that all of them "seem to be ignorant of any other sense than 'turning' for this word."[25]

In a later work, Bushnell traces the change from "turning" to "desire" to an obscure mid-sixteenth-century Dominican monk, Pagnino, and she notes that between Wycliffe's translation and Coverdale's the translation was changed, and has been followed since.[26] She looks at other uses of this word in the Old and New Testaments and finds that indeed the sense is that of turning.[27] Citing Bushnell, Maxwell agrees with this and with her change of "shall" to "will."[28] For Bushnell, the difference is that the rule of the husband over wife is not a punishment meted out by God in payment for Eve's disobedience, but is the result of her turning away from God to follow her husband.[29] However, most modern translations of the Bible render *teshuqa* as "desire" or a similar term, and translate it as the imperative form of the verb: "shall desire."[30]

In this same passage, Trible's translation also eschews the imperative. However, she does translate *teshuqa* as "desire": "For your man is your desire, but he will rule over you." Her explanation is that Eve "still yearns for the original unity of male and female"[31] which because of the division of flesh caused by the disobedience cannot be. Trible and Bushnell are in accord that "[Man's] supremacy is neither a divine right nor a male prerogative. [Woman's] subordination is neither a divine decree nor a female destiny. Both their positions result from shared disobedi-

---

24 Bushnell, *God's Word to Women,* par. 129.
25 Ibid., additional note, par. 144.
26 Bushnell, *Reverend Doctor,* 68, 71–73.
27 Bushnell, *God's Word to Women,* lessons 17–18, par. 130.
28 Maxwell, *Women in Ministry,* 38.
29 Bushnell, *God's Word to Women,* par. 122–24.
30 Modern translations of the Bible using the imperative "shall" are KJV, RSV, NAB, NEB; NIV and NJB show "will." Other words used instead of "desire" are "eager" (NEB), "yearning" (JB).
31 Trible, *God and the Rhetoric of Sexuality,* 127, 128.

ence. God describes this consequence but does not prescribe it as punishment."[32] This view receives ample support. Benno says that "I will greatly multiply . . ." is not correctly interpreted as punishment. He finds no command that man be master and woman servant.[33] Aschkenasy says that "man and woman are equally culpable in the eyes of God, and equally responsible for the consequences of their deed."[34]

Bushnell concluded that she had convincingly destroyed the basis used by scholars since 1528 to subordinate women. "In clearing up this passage by exposing its garbled sense, [the way has been fully cleared] as to the right of women to equality with men, in the Church. . . . There can be no sufficient grounds upon which to base the doctrine of the subordination of woman to man, unless Genesis three-sixteen stands as to its traditional interpretation." For Bushnell, it does not so stand. Any punishment for the woman comes when she turns away from God to the man, and it is only at this point that she falls under man's rule.[35]

All of this works out, for Bushnell, with the authority resting in whichever of the married couple is closest to "the right moral view,"[36] and this theme appears again and again in her work. Men and women must be equally moral, equally pure. Where impurity exists, each should shoulder the same shame and punishment. Bushnell never suggests that the male alone should carry the blame, but that both partners share equally.[37]

1 Corinthians 14:33–36

Although Bushnell dealt with a number of New Testament passages, the ones to which she gave the most detailed treatment in both *God's Word to Women* and *The Reverend Doctor and His Doctor Daughter* are found in 1 Corinthians. For Bushnell, both

---

32 Ibid.; Bushnell, *God's Word to Women*, par. 68–74. Bushnell expresses the same general thought.

33 Jacob Benno, *The First Book of the Bible: Genesis* (New York: Ktav, 1974), 29–30.

34 Aschkenasy, *Eve's Journey*, 11.

35 Bushnell, *Reverend Doctor*, 71, 74–75; quotation is on p. 71.

36 Bushnell, *God's Word to Women*, par. 150.

37 Ibid., par. 443, 421, 447, 458, 573, etc.

veiling and keeping silence in church are symbolic of the requirement of subordination of women. She feels she has refuted this
requirement by her reinterpretation of the passages in Genesis,
and in her new interpretations of the passages in 1 Corinthians,
she intends to show that Paul agrees.

What part should women play in the life of the church? This
issue continues to ignite theological discussion, and although it
is seldom acknowledged, Bushnell's interpretation is being "discovered" by scholars.[38] As more women answer their calls to
ordained ministry, the question of women's keeping silence in
the church is one that must be answered. In an article in the 12
September 1889 issue of *The Union Signal,* Bushnell provided an
answer in the context of a Bible lesson. (See the appendix for the
text of the article.)

Bushnell begins her answer by pointing out the inconsistency that in 1 Corinthians 14:31 (AV), Paul has allowed that "ye
may all prophesy, one by one, that all may learn, and all may be
comforted," and she notes the triple occurrence of the word "all."
Bushnell then looks at 14:34 itself—"It is not permitted . . . as also
saith the law"—and asks "What law?"[39] Neither Old Testament
nor New Testament has any such law; to the contrary, women are
permitted to speak.

Bushnell discusses various attempts to reconcile Paul's per-
mission for all to prophesy and for women to keep silence: 1) this
is only a local prohibition; 2) Paul changes his mind (quickly);
3) Paul forbids babbling and chattering but not prophesying; and
4) Paul is only forbidding questions.[40] These same attempts at
resolution are still made by scholars, but Bushnell's objections
to these attempts are also supported by other present-day interpreters.

Some scholars who support the first attempt to resolve this
tension—that this is a local prohibition—are Orr and Walther,
who relate the prohibition to other disorders in the Corinthian
church;[41] Keir, who sees this situation as "clearly a local problem"

---

38 Dowd, "Old Roots," 1.
39 Bushnell, *God's Word to Women,* par. 190, 191.
40 Ibid., par. 197.
41 William F. Orr and James Arthur Walther, *1 Corinthians,* vol. 32 of

where Paul is ordering "the Corinthian feminists to be silent without affecting their basic right of taking an audible part in congregational worship in an orderly fashion";[42] and Martin, who has determined that the women were teaching gnostic heresy and therefore their teaching had to be silenced.[43] Bushnell's only reply here is to warn against weakening scriptural authority by such restriction to locale, although she allows that this sometimes occurs.[44]

The second attempt at resolution—that Paul changed his mind—has been supported by Koenig, who finds Paul satisfied to have "an unresolved tension in [his] thought,"[45] and MacGorman, who finds that Paul has done the same elsewhere (1 Cor. 8:4–6; 10:21).[46] Bushnell replies that if Paul changed his mind, he changed it quickly, and suggests that this would not occur under the guidance of the Holy Spirit. Martin also doubts that Paul would contradict himself so quickly.[47]

The third argument—that Paul is forbidding only babbling and chattering—finds more support among modern critical scholars. Thrall says that the tension should be resolved by understanding that Paul is referring here to anything other than prayer or prophecy.[48] Foh thinks that this is the "most reasonable

the Anchor Bible, ed. William Foxwell Albright and David Noel Freedman (Garden City, NY: Doubleday, 1976), 313.

42　J. Howard Keir, "Neither Male nor Female: An Examination of the Status of Women in the New Testament," *Evangelical Quarterly* 55 (1983): 38.

43　Martin suggests that women teachers (1 Tim. 2:8–15) were "possibly Gnostics" and he links the passages in Timothy with 1 Corinthians 14:34 by "its language" (87). Ralph P. Martin, *The Spirit and the Congregation: Studies in 1 Corinthians 12–15* (Grand Rapids: Eerdmans, 1984), 86–87.

44　Bushnell, *God's Word to Women*, par. 197.

45　John Koenig, *Charismata: God's Gifts for God's People* (Philadelphia: Westminster, 1978), 174.

46　Jack M. MacGorman, *The Gifts of the Spirit: An Exposition of 1 Corinthians 12–14* (Nashville: Broadman, 1974), 113.

47　Martin, *Spirit and Congregation*, 84.

48　Margaret E. Thrall, *I and II Corinthians* (Cambridge: Cambridge

theory."[49] Morris cites Moffatt, who agrees that 14:34 excludes prayer and prophecy.[50] Bushnell objects to this argument on the grounds that while Paul uses this form of the word *lalein* twenty-three times in this chapter, he never uses it to mean "chattering" or "babbling" but rather "solemn utterance under Divine inspiration."[51] She also does not find adequate proof that the women were chattering or babbling to begin with. Carson's interpretation agrees with this part of Bushnell's and asks why: Even if some were babbling, would Paul silence all the women?[52]

Morris suggests that Paul is reminding the Corinthians of the law.[53] Bushnell's objections to this argument is that there is no such Torah law and that Paul would not cite Jewish Talmudic law.[54] Fee agrees both that "the Law does *not* say any such thing" and that "under any view this is difficult to reconcile with Paul."[55]

To the final argument—that Paul is only forbidding questions—Bushnell first asks whether we know if even men asked questions in church, and then asks how single women and women married to pagan or Jewish husbands would have their questions answered.[56] Robertson and Plummer posit that unmarried women (and presumably those married to heathens) would ask their questions of married women, who can then question their husbands at home and circulate the answers.[57] Bushnell does not deal with this specific possibility, but she feels that such

---

University Press, 1965), 102.

49 Susan T. Foh, *Women and the Word of God: A Response to Biblical Feminism* (Phillipsburg, NJ: Presbyterian and Reformed, 1979), 119.

50 Leon Morris, *First Epistle to the Corinthians* (Grand Rapids: Eerdmans, 1958), 201.

51 Bushnell, *God's Word to Women*, par. 197.

52 Carson, *Showing the Spirit*, 138.

53 Morris, *First Epistle to the Corinthians*, 201.

54 Bushnell, *God's Word to Women*, 191, 200–202.

55 Fee, *First Epistle to the Corinthians*, 707. Fee does not cite Bushnell in his opinion here.

56 Bushnell, *God's Word to Women*, par. 197.

57 A. T. Robertson and Alfred Plummer, *A Critical and Exegetical Commentary on the First Epistle of St. Paul to the Corinthians* (New York: Charles Scribner's Sons, 1911), 325.

a prohibition would leave many women starved for the Word. She concludes that most of the Bible will be for men only, if women are to keep silence.[58]

Therefore, Bushnell sees "it is not permitted" as coming from outside Scripture, not from within it, and probably from Jewish oral tradition: "we are driven to believe the Apostle was not uttering his own views in verses 34 and 35 of 1 Cor. 14. . . ." Paul is quoting the assertion of Judaizers here, and his response is "What! came the word of God out from you? or came it unto you only?"[59] Bushnell then quotes the authorities of her time, such as Sir William Ramsay, who says:

> We should be ready to suspect Paul is making a quotation from the letter addressed to him by the Corinthians whenever he alludes to their knowledge, or when any statement stands in marked contrast either with the immediate context or with Paul's known views.[60]

Evans also discusses the various "misfits" discussed by Bushnell, and Evans finds similar reasons for the "misfits." She then offers Bushnell's argument that Paul is quoting from a letter or the opinion of a particular group. Either this is the case, says Evans, or Paul is discouraging the practice of "wives taking part in the public discussion of prophesies made by their own husbands."[61] Mickelsen sees the same two possibilities: that wives are interrupting or that Paul is quoting the Judaizers.[62] Neither Mickelsen nor Evans cites Bushnell, but their arguments develop along the same lines. Bushnell, of course, contends—as do an increasing number of modern scholars—that Paul does permit women to speak, and does so immediately prior to his quote from the letter in verse 31: "You can all prophesy one by one . . ."

Bushnell completes her argument with the conclusion that to interpret Paul's words as a stricture against women prophesying is to make Paul contradict himself in a ridiculous manner: "Let

58 Bushnell, *God's Word to Women*, par. 200.
59 Ibid., par. 203.
60 Ibid., par. 205.
61 Evans, *Woman in the Bible*, 95–100.
62 Mickelsen, "An Egalitarian View," in *Women in Ministry*, 198–99.

the women keep silence . . . wherefore covet to prophesy. . . . Let the women keep silence . . . wherefore forbid not to speak."[63] Paul is not forbidding, but is sincerely howing the error of those in Corinth who hold to the Jewish law, exposing the motive as jealousy and then ordering that "all things be done decently and in order" (1 Cor. 34:40).[64]

1 Corinthians 11:10

Having promised earlier to contest both quotations—1 Corinthians 14:34–36 and 1 Corinthians 11:1–16—Bushnell now turns her attention to the latter in lessons 29–35: "The Sophistry of the Veil."[65] She finds various "misfits," one of the most important of which being that in verse 10 the word "power" is translated as "symbol of subjection."[66] Bushnell translates this "ought to have power over her head." This interpretation of *exousia* is common in critical scholarship. Morris and Bushnell both cite Ramsay's scorn for the idea of *exousia* as a symbol of subjection; Ramsay writes that it is a "preposterous idea which a Greek scholar would laugh at anywhere except in the N.T."[67] Liefeld cites the same passage in Ramsay, seeing efforts to discount this as failing to "pick up signals from the text itself that counter the traditions about restricting women."[68] Ramsay and Morris agree that the veil gives a woman power to function freely in the society of Paul's time, without which she would be viewed as a disrepu-

---

63 Bushnell, *God's Word to Women,* par. 210.

64 Hans Conzelmann, *1 Corinthians,* ed. George W. MacRae, trans. James W. Leitch (Philadelphia: Fortress, 1975), 246. Conzelmann and many other scholars argue on the basis of the textual variants that 1 Corinthians 14:33–36 is an interpolation and should not be included. Bushnell did not consider the text-critical problem.

65 Bushnell, *God's Word to Women,* par. 216–70.

66 Bushnell (par. 216) is quoting from Weymouth's Modern English translation.

67 Morris, *First Epistle to the Corinthians,* 154; Bushnell, *God's Word to Women,* par. 220.

68 Walter L. Liefeld, "A Plural Ministry Response" to "A Traditional View" in *Women in Ministry,* 57–58.

table person. Morris feels that though the context indicates something like "a symbol of subjection," the Greek word means rather "a sign of her authority."[69] This is also the sense that Bushnell favors.[70]

Bushnell also finds support among more contemporary evangelicals. Evans finds "no warrant at all for the replacement, as in the RSV, of *exousia* by the word veil," and she notes others who agree: Hurley and Banks, both of whom see women's authority recognized as legitimate in this passage. Again, while Evans does not cite Bushnell, their arguments are similar.[71] Hull indicates that *exousia* simply means authority, and gives a literal translation of verse 10 (similar to Bushnell's): "the woman ought to have authority on her head." Hull also says that this is only one of many arguments, and that textual variants confuse the issue.[72] Mickelson finds this one more instance of "translators letting their personal beliefs get in the way of the text,"[73] a finding with which Bushnell would heartily agree.

Conzelmann also deals at length with the meaning of *exousia*. In his discussion he cites Kittel, who says that the word translated as "headband" in Aramaic could be derived from the Aramaic word translated as "to exercise power." He then quotes Kummel as saying that this is impossible as it would infer that "Paul would have erroneously (!) rendered an Aramaic word by means of a Greek one which cannot designate any kind of headgear; and that Greek readers would not have been able to understand him."[74] Bushnell's argument is similar: ". . . to pretend that [Paul] knew how to *argue* a point, but could not *express* the point, is puerile. Whether Paul knew how to argue clearly or not, he knew how to state what he was arguing about . . ."[75] Conzelmann asserts that the headcovering or veil must "represent a protec-

---

69 Morris, *First Epistle to the Corinthians*, 153.
70 Bushnell, *God's Word to Women*, par. 216–18.
71 Evans, *Woman in the Bible*, 91.
72 Hull, *Equal to Serve*, 254–55.
73 Mickelsen, "An Egalitarian View," in *Women in Ministry*, 197.
74 Conzelmann, *1 Corinthians*, 189.
75 Bushnell, *God's Word to Women*, par. 219.

tive power" but asks "against whom?"[76] This is the question Bushnell also asks.[77]

Bushnell is forthright in her conclusions about the majority of her contemporary male translators and expositors. "The truth is, had some of these expositors been one-tenth as broad as St. Paul on the 'woman question,' and honest besides, we should never have been taught these pitiful, puerile, and ego-centric perversions of Paul's meaning."[78]

The foregoing is only a taste of what Bushnell's work has to offer. She deals with a number of other "misfits" and with many other controversial biblical passages in both Old and New Testaments. The views she holds have found both support and criticism in subsequent research and there continues to be much profit in studying Bushnell's work. The concluding chapter of this study will look at the impact and value of her work for today.

---

76 Conzelmann, *1 Corinthians*, 189.
77 Bushnell, *God's Word to Women*, par. 218.
78 Ibid., par. 239.

CONCLUSION

I n reading and evaluating Bushnell's work, the reader needs to be cognizant of several factors: the state of the art of biblical exegesis in her day, the Victorian era from which she sprang, the position of women in the late nineteenth and early twentieth centuries, and the materials she would have available to her in her independent study of the Bible and biblical languages. Bushnell deplored the state of affairs which did not permit women to study in the seminaries and universities.[1] A constant theme in her writings was the call for women as well as men to educate themselves in the biblical languages and to take part in the work of biblical translation and interpretation so that each could serve as a buffer against the bias of the other. While she believed in the infallibility of the Bible, she felt that

> criticism of a Bible exposition may be undertaken in the inter-
> ests of a deeper reverence for the Word than the expositor who
> is criticized has shown. . . . We hold the Bible as supreme in
> authority, and its text as inviolable. But we must not forget that
> man's prattle about it may be very foolish.[2]

Bushnell saw the task of educated women as twofold.[3] First, they must spread to all women in all places the full gospel message of the same freedom and equality as men have in Jesus Christ. She found particular warrants for women's preaching the

---

1 Bushnell, *Reverend Doctor,* 126.
2 Katharine Bushnell, *The Badge of Guilt and Shame* (Oakland, CA: By the author, n.d.), 7.
3 Bushnell, *Reverend Doctor,* 130.

Good News in three passages: Joel 2:28–29 (KJV), "And also upon the servants and upon the handmaids in those days will I pour out my spirit"; Psalm 68:11 (RV), "The Lord giveth the word; the women that publish the tidings are a great host"; and Isaiah 40:9, which Bushnell translates as "Oh thou woman that bringest good tidings to Zion . . . to Jerusalem . . . say unto the cities of Judah, Behold your God."[4] She wanted women who were called to preach to take their place in the pulpit, as she saw the early Christian women doing, "from Anna onward . . . as the good news came to them."[5] She herself did so whenever possible.[6]

Second, educated women must attack the "false teachings as to the place of women in God's economy" and break the "tyranny of the 'traditions' of the elders" found in commentaries.[7] The problem in the "tradition" was the consistent bias toward male preference shown by male translators wherever there was the possibility of a choice. "Why," she asked, "should fossilized theologians be allowed to drag their antiquated notions across the pages of every biblical commentary which is published for the use of Christians?"[8] She devoted the last forty years of her life to the task of breaking this tradition. Bushnell believed that fulfillment of these two tasks would strengthen the "faith of women in the Word by correcting the teachings on the 'woman question;' and the faith of others, too, who have felt the apparent injustice to woman that the Bible seemed to teach."[9]

---

4   Bushnell, *God's Word to Women*, par. 209, 717, 773, 792, 826. Bushnell claims that "there is precisely the same warrant, from the original Hebrew, for inserting 'woman' in this passage in Isaiah, as there is for inserting 'woman' . . . in Psalm 68:11." (826).

5   Ibid., par. 792.

6   Mrs. G. C. Smith, "Social Purity Work," *The Union Signal* 13 (5 May 1887), 12 (WCTU microfilm edition), roll 4, frame 149; L. Anna Ballard, "Dr. Bushnell's Good Work," *The Union Signal* 14 (25 October 1888), 12 (WCTU microfilm edition), roll 5, frame 219. Both preaching engagements were in Methodist Episcopal churches: the first in Springfield, Illinois, and the second in Lansing, Michigan.

7   Bushnell, *Reverend Doctor,* 125.

8   Bushnell, *God's Word to Women,* par. 275.

9   Ibid., 126.

Bushnell's experience with women in nearly every country of the world enabled her to see relationships between women as a healing agent and a positive force for world peace. She saw international hatred at the root of the evils she combatted in her crusades. "One reason why Dr. Bushnell look[ed] so hopefully upon . . . women's work is because it [was] so easy for women to love one another."[10]

There are a number of authors whose work closely follows Bushnell's, although in at least one no credit is given. Jessie Penn-Lewis found *God's Word to Women* so valuable that she condensed it into a smaller volume and had it published in England with Bushnell's approval and blessing.[11] Starr bases much of her thinking on Bushnell in *The Bible Status of Woman*, and cites Bushnell freely in her treatments of critical passages in Genesis, Corinthians, and 1 Timothy. She also is one with Bushnell in her belief that "diverse weights and measures" were used in translation, depending on whether or not what was being translated referred to men or women.[12] Maxwell also acknowledges his debt to Bushnell's work.[13]

One work that appears to be dependent on Bushnell is Helen Barrett Montgomery's *Centenary Translation of the New Testament*. Sharyn Dowd has presented convincing evidence that Montgomery has strong (but unacknowledged) dependence on Bushnell in the passages from 1 Corinthians 14 and 1 Corinthians 11, both in her exegesis and in the authorities she quotes; and, according to Dowd, Montgomery changed her view on Corinthians to match Bushnell's.[14]

Katharine Bushnell was far ahead of her time. Comparisons of her work with that of current scholars show her to be on the cutting edge of many biblical issues debated today. Bushnell is an important example of how visions outside the academic power structure go unheeded in spite of their perspicacious insights. Ray

---

10 Mary A. Ward Poole, "English Farewells," *The Union Signal* 19 (14 September 1893), 5 (WCTU microfilm edition), roll 9, frame 140.

11 Penn-Lewis, *"Magna Charta" of Woman;* see chap. 7.

12 Starr, *Bible Status of Women,* 20, 28, 43–44, 311–12, 264–65.

13 Maxwell, *Women in Ministry.*

14 Dowd, "Old Roots," 5–6, 7.

Munson, the Pentecostal preacher responsbile for recovering *God's Word to Women* from the depths into which it had disappeared, criticizes her in his foreword to the reprint edition:

> I know that Sister Bushnell at times conveys thoughts . . . that can be misleading, especially where she suggests that the first five books of the Bible could have been produced by oral history repeated down through successive generations by the overlapping lives of the contemporaries of each generation and culminating in Moses writing the historical account excepting the account of his own cessation of earth ministry. Also where she suggests that the flood might have covered only the known world in Noah's day.[15]

Few biblical scholars today would debate that Bushnell's observations have more than a kernel of truth. This ninteenth-century woman was stating positions that have come into consideration only in the past few decades. A thorough study of all her work needs to be done to explore what other new and exciting interpretations may remain to be called out of the depths.

Bushnell stands for the freedom and equality of all women everywhere. She stands for the right and responsibility of women to take their position beside men and to be heard in every arena of life. She stands for the responsibility of women to educate themselves adequately to fulfill their responsibility and she looks with contempt on those who would shun that responsibility.

In the final paragraph of *God's Word to Women,* Bushnell flings a final challenge to all women:

> To which body will we belong? That is the question for each woman to answer to herself. . . . A great promise and prophecy—the very greatest in all the Bible—lies before us women. We cannot escape; we must either choose the best that could be, from

---

15 Ray Munson, foreword, in Bushnell, *God's Word to Women.* In the foreword, Munson admits to having "deleted from the author's text, in a part of one paragraph, where I felt it could pose a problem of misunderstanding in the minds of some . . ." He does not indicate which paragraph was deleted.

the highest standpoint, or by failing to choose prove ourselves [unworthy of our birthright]. God has given the challenge to our faith. Shall we despise our birthright? God forbid![16]

Bushnell met her own challenge. She rejoiced in the promise and prophecy she found through her study and reinterpretation of Scripture. She claimed the birthright and fulfilled the promise. Katharine Bushell's life and work stand as example and monument to that fulfullment—

"Oh thou woman that bringest good tidings!"

---

16 Bushnell, *God's Word to Women*, par. 839.

APPENDIX: "KEEP SILENCE"

By Kate C. Bushnell, M.D.

G entle reader, supposing you get out your Bible, and we will
have a lesson together, this morning. Turn, please, to I. Cor.
14:31–40.

Now the male commentator [notes] two verses in that passage that are of infinitely more importance to him than all the
rest in the passage put together. They are the thirty-fourth and
thirty-fifth. To maintain the dignity of his translation of these two
verses, he is quite in the habit of plunging right into the middle
of that section, making chaos of everything else, that he may, by
sheer masculine force, keep the verses plumb to his ideas of
womanly uprightness. Do you agree with me in that assertion? If
not, let me illustrate my point.

Let us compare verses 31 and 34.

{31} "Ye can all prophesy one by one." / {34} "Let your women
keep silence."

Why does not Paul note and explain the inconsistency here?

Now let us try verses 32 and 34.

{32} "The spirits of the prophets are subject to the prophets."
{34} "Let them [the women] be in subjection" [to their hus-
bands].

But Paul knew and recognized *women* prophets, and women
prophets in Corinth, too: see I. Cor. 11:5.

Now does Paul mean, after all, that it is the spirit of the *male*
prophet only that is to be subject to the prophet? and that the
spirit of the female prophet is subject to her husband? And,

supposing, as not at all unlikely, this husband is still a heathen, and a *Corinthian* heathen at that. Then the Divine spirit in a prophetess is to be controlled and guided by the devilish spirit of a Corinthian heathen. Why does not Paul explain this great inconsistency, or even mention the fact that by prophet he means *male* prophet only?

Now compare verses 36 and 35.

{36} "What, was it from you [men] that the Word of God went forth, or came it unto you [men] alone?" / {35} "It is shameful for a woman to speak in the church."

Let us consider the construction of this thirty-sixth verse a moment. Is there any warrant for inserting, as explanatory, the word *men* in two places, as I have done in this instance? I think there is, for the following reasons:

In the English language we use *alone* and *only* interchangeably (although incorrectly); not so the Greek. This word translated *only* in the Old Version is changed to *alone* in the New, because *only* could be an adverb qualifying come, while in fact the word used is an adjective qualifying men understood. Oh, how easily a preconception can introduce error into a translation of this Holy Word! This adjective is in the masculine gender—a matter of considerable import just here. It gives full warrant for the introduction of the word men as explanatory of the thought. But, you object, by such a rule of translation as that, then we would need to declare that *brethren* in the twenty-sixth verse, and *man* in the twenty-seventh, etc., relate to males only, while you are trying to show the very opposite.

I hardly admit it. Had the adjective *alone* been correctly translated as in the Old Version by *only*, such might be the case. But when Paul asks, "What, came the Word of God unto you men when you were alone by yourselves?" it is perfectly plain that in the very question he implies the presence of others besides these comprehended in the word (masculine) you. Does he refer then to Timothy, Titus, the Thessalonians, or to whom? Common sense tells us that he refers to another class *not* remote from his present consideration at all, or he would say to whom. Hence when he exclaims so emphatically that the word did not come to "you" alone, he meant just what the Bible teaches, viz.: that the word came unto *women* also. [See Acts 1st and 2d chapters.]

Now let us compare verses 39 and 34 and see if they are consistent.

{39} "Wherefore, my brethren forbid not to speak with tongues." / {34} "Let your women keep silence in the churches."

To what does this *wherefore* refer? and of what is it the conclusion?

It refers either to verses 34 and 36, or else to some others. Let us couple it first with 34 and 35, and see if it makes an intelligible statement:

"Let your women keep silence."

"Let them ask their husbands at home."

"It is a shame for them to speak."

"Let them be in subjection; wherefore forbid not to speak with tongues."

Well, *that* would make more sense if we made the conclusion of the whole matter be "wherefore *forbid women* to speak with tongues," and more truthful, too. Hence the "wherefore" is not a conclusion derived from verses 34 and 35.

Let us now couple this summing up of the argument to all the rest of the verses. "All can prophesy." (31.)

"The spirits of prophets are subject to prophets." (32.)

"God is not a God of confusion, but of peace." (33.)

"The Word did not go forth from men." (36.)

"The word did not come unto men alone." (37.)

Now couple Paul's "wherefore" with each one of these verses, and we see nothing but beautiful consistency everywhere. Try it yourself, and see! Well! that, I admit, disjoints verses 34 and 35 from all the rest of this passage. Yes, and I believe it should be so disjointed. I believe it would have been so disjointed by male commentators had it related to limitations on the male sex. But man has invented the remarkable theory that while "God is no respecter of persons," still God does respect bifurcated garments worn by persons. Souls, God treats alike; sexes, He treats very differently.

Let us make Paul his own interpreter. Turn to I. Cor. 15:29–34. Supposing an epicurean or an annihilist wished to establish his pet theory, he would not need to overturn the authority of as many verses to teach that we must give ourselves to eating and drinking to-day because death ends everything. I say he would not need to overturn the authority of as many adjacent Scripture verses to set up that one clause, as the male commentator must overthrow to set up as of divine authority the sentences beginning, "Let your women keep silence."

But the male commentator says: "'Let us eat and drink, for to-morrow we die,' are supposed to be the words of another reasoning with Paul."

Yes, and why not admit that the verses beginning, "Let the women keep silence," is also the voice of an objector? Haven't we some reason for so thinking, when Paul says it is the *law* saying it? He tells where the objector springs from—those sticklers for *law* who were always contending with Paul; and Paul declares his impatience with them by his exclamation: "What! was it from you *men* that the word came? isn't God's authority higher than your law? Remember that the word didn't even come upon you men alone. If you think yourself a prophet, you will be able to discern that these things are from the Lord; but if you are an ignorant pretender, you will have to remain such."

"Wherefore, don't forbid these women to speak with tongues. Let everything be done decently and in order."

Now, my dear sister, the lesson is over, excepting one question I want you to think about with me: Shall we ignore all the force there is in the admonitions contained in eight verses of these ten in the lesson, in order to force a meaning into the remaining two that will suit the male commentator? I do not think that is treating Paul and Scripture with proper reverence, do you?

(The original article appeared in *The Union Signal* 15 [12 September 1889], 7. It is available in the WCTU microfilm edition, roll 5, frame 609.)

BIBLIOGRAPHY

Annotated Bibliography

of Katharine C. Bushnell

(in chronological order, undated material first)

꽝

undated. *The Badge of Guilt and Shame*. Oakland, CA: By the author. Exegesis and interpretation of 1 Corinthians 11:3–16 on the veiling of women in worship. 53 pages with appendix on history of translation change of *exousia* from "power" to "veil." Available at Lexington Theologicl Seminary, Lexington, Kentucky.

undated. *Covet to Prophesy*. Oakland, CA: By the author. Interpretation of 1 Corinthians 14:34, "Let the woman keep silence," positing this as a Corinthian slogan. Shows Paul not in favor of women keeping silence. 37 pages. Whereabouts unknown.

c. 1887. *The Woman Condemned*. New York: Funk & Wagnalls. Deals with the consequences of the double standard of morality for men and women prevalent in contemporary society. One of a series of leaflets. Whereabouts unknown.

1888a. "Law and Social Purity." *The Union Signal* 14 (22 November), 2–3 (National Headquarters, WCTU [Joint Ohio Historical Society—Michigan Historical Collections—WCTU microfilm edition], roll 5, frame 250. All entries cited from WCTU microfilm edition are from this collection). An argument for the change of the laws of sexual consent, particularly with reference to their use in rape trials for the defense of confessed rapists.

1888b. "Work in Northern Wisconsin." *W.C.T.U. State Work* (Madison, Wisconsin) 3 (November): 1–7. Full report of Bushnell's crusade against prostitution in Wisconsin as delivered to the National WCTU Convention. Available at Lexington Theological Seminary, Lexington, Kentucky.

1889a. "The Facts in the Case." *The Union Signal* 15 (7 March), 5 (WCTU microfilm edition), roll 5, frame 382. Gives the facts of crusade in Wisconsin to refute exaggerated and embellished newspaper stories.

1889b. "Mrs. Josephine Butler." *The Union Signal* 15 (26 December), 10 (WCTU microfilm edition), roll 6, frame 107. Biography of Josephine Butler telling of her difficulties in her ministry to prostitutes.

1894a. "An Appeal to Purity Workers." *The Union Signal* 20 (29 March), 5 (WCTU microfilm edition), roll 9, frame 10. Appeal against the regulation of prostitution in Cleveland, Ohio. Gives information about the crusade in India against state regulation and about the battle in Parliament for repeal of the Contagious Diseases Acts.

1894b. "Answer to Dr. Lyman Abbott." *The Union Signal* 20 (WCTU microfilm edition), roll 9. Series in three parts: (7 June), 3–4, frames 490–91; (14 June), 2–3, frame 498; (21 June), 2, frame 507. Exegesis of Ephesians 5:21–24, refuting the claims of Dr. Lyman Abbott that in this passage Paul is dealing only with married pairs, that husbands have the right to command wives, and that the husband is the final authority.

1895. "When Doctors Disagree." *The Union Signal* 21 (WCTU microfilm edition), roll 10. Series in three parts: (3 January) 3; (10 January), 4; (17 January), 3. Refutes the interpretation of 1 Corinthians 11 of the requirement that women veil in worship.

1896. *A Clean Life*. Chicago: Women's Temperance Publishing Association. Teaches personal and matrimonial principles from the viewpoint of Christian purity. Subjects treated: "Dead Unto Sin—Alive Unto God," "The Law of Love," "The Appetites," "A Holy Seed," "Communion With God," "Clean Impulses," and "Clean Thoughts." Whereabouts unknown.

1899. and Elizabeth W. Andrew. *The Queen's Daughters in India.* London: Morgan & Scott. Story of Bushnell's and Andrew's campaign in India to expose and eliminate regulation of vice in the British military cantonments. 127 pages. Available at Lexington Theological Seminary, Lexington, Kentucky.

1907. and Elizabeth W. Andrew. *Heathen Slaves and Christian Rulers.* Oakland, CA: Messiah's Advocate. Traces the history of forced prostitution in Hong Kong, China, and San Francisco. Contains several accounts of rescues of slave-prostitutes from San Francisco brothels by rescue mission workers. Available at Lexington Theological Seminary, Lexington, Kentucky; University of Oregon Library.

1910, 1912, 1914. *101 Questions Answered: A Woman's Catechism.* Southport, England: Lowes Limited. Covers Old Testament interpretation in first fifty lessons of *God's Word to Women.* Set in a question-and-answer style. 73 pages. Available at Lexington Theological Seminary, Lexington, Kentucky.

1916, 1921, 1923, 1930. *God's Word to Women: One Hundred Bible Studies on Woman's Place in the Divine Economy.* Oakland, CA: By the author. Explores passages in the Old and New Testaments of particular interest to women, especially those in Genesis and 1 Corinthians. Gives nontraditional interpretations of these passages with the view to encourage women to take their rightful place in ministry and Christian living. Approximately 400 pages. Available from two sources: Ray Munson, 11899 Gowanda Road, North Collins, NY 14111; Bernice Menold, 10303 North Spring Lane, Peoria, IL 61615.

1919. "What's Going On? A Report of Investigation by Katharine C. Bushnell, M.D., regarding certain legal abuses in California that have been in part aggravated and in part created by the Federal Social Hygiene Program." Oakland, CA: By the author.

36 pages. Available at Lexington Theological Seminary, Lexington, Kentucky.

1924. *The Supreme Virtue: Loyalty to God's Anointed King.* Oakland, CA: Katharine C. Bushnell. A unique literal interpretation of the Song of Solomon with Abishag and Adonijah as the lovers. 58 pages. Available at Lexington Theological Seminary, Lexington, Kentucky.

1927. *The Reverend Doctor and His Doctor Daughter.* Oakland, CA: By the author. A much lighter and frequently humorous reworking of *God's Word to Women,* which takes the form of a conversation between a stuffy, opinionated minister father and his medically trained but pulpit-called daughter. 133 pages. Available at Lexington Theological Seminary, Lexington, Kentucky.

1932. *Dr. Katharine C. Bushnell: A Brief Sketch of Her Life Work.* Hertford, England: Rose & Sons. Originally appeared as a series of articles for the *Biblical Record,* an Australian periodical, later published as a single unit in England. Story of Bushnell's life and work from college until about 1930. A "Supplementary Chapter" that was not included in the original series was added before publication in England. This pamphlet concentrates on her work in India, but gives many personal details of her life. Few dates are given. 29 pages. Available at Lexington Theological Seminary, Lexington, Kentucky.

1938a. *Mother's Catechism on Adam and Eve.* Piedmont, Oakland, CA: By the author. Spinoff from *God's Word to Women.* Exegesis and interpretation of Genesis 3. 58 pages. Available at Lexington Theological Seminary, Lexington, Kentucky.

1938b. *Mother's Catechism on The Seventh of First Corinthians.* Piedmont, Oakland, CA: By the author. An interpretation of 1 Corinthians 7 designed to refute the argument that this chapter is a set of general rules for matrimonial behavior. Bushnell contends that its purpose is to give advice for the conduct of the husband during times of persecution. 46 pages. Available at Lexington Theological Seminary, Lexington, Kentucky.

1945. *The Vashti-Esther Bible Story.* Piedmont, CA: By the author. An interpretation of the Book of Esther, particularly of four acrostics spelling out "Yahweh" and one spelling "I AM." Explores the significance of these acrostics. 32 pages. Available at Lexington Theological Seminary, Lexington, Kentucky.

Secondary Sources

Allison, Robert W. "Let Women Be Silent in the Churches (1 Cor 14:33b–36): What Did Paul Really Say, And What Did It Mean?" *Journal for the Study of the New Testament* 32 (1988): 27–60.

Anderson, John A. *Women's Warfare and Ministry; What Saith the Scriptures?* Stonehaven, Great Britain: David Waldie, 1933.

Andrew, Elizabeth Wheeler. "A Winter's Purity Campaign in India." *The Union Signal* 19 (11 May 1893), 2 (National Headquarters, WCTU [Joint Ohio Historical Society—Michigan Historical Collections—WCTU microfilm edition]), roll 8, frame 578. All entries cited from either Frances Willard WCTU Scrapbook or the microfilm edition are from this microfilm collection.

Aschkenasy, Nehama. *Eve's Journey: Feminine Images in Hebraic Literary Tradition.* Philadelphia: University of Pennsylvania Press, 1986.

Ballard, L. Anna. "Dr. Bushnell's Good Work." *The Union Signal* 14 (25 October 1888), 12 (WCTU microfilm edition), roll 5, frame 219.

Bell, Enid Hester Chataway Moberly. *Josephine Butler: Flame of Fire.* London: Constable and Co., Ltd., 1962.

Benno, Jacob. *The First Book of the Bible: Genesis.* New York: Ktav, 1974.

Bilezikian, Gilbert. *Beyond Sex Roles.* Grand Rapids: Baker, 1985.

Bridges, Linda M. "Silencing the Corinthian Men, Not the Women." In *The New Has Come: Emerging Roles among Southern Baptist Women,* ed. Anne Thomas Neil and Virginia Garrett

Neely, 40–49. Washington, D.C.: Southern Baptist Alliance, 1989.

British Museum General Catalogue of Printed Books to 1955. Vol. 4. Compact ed. New York: Readex Microprint Corporation, 1967.

Bullard, R. A. "Feminine and Feminist Touches in the Centenary New Testament." *The Bible Translator* 38 (1987): 118–22.

"Bushnell Rites Set for Monday." *Oakland Tribune,* 27 January 1946. Photocopy of obituary sent by manager of Truman's Funeral Directors to Ruth Hoppin.

Butler, Arthur S. G. *Portrait of Josephine Butler.* London: Faber and Faber Ltd., 1954.

Butler, Josephine E. *Personal Reminiscences of a Great Crusade.* London: Horace Marshall & Son, 1911; reprint, Westport, Connecticut: Hyperion, 1976.

Carson, D. A. *Showing the Spirit: A Theological Exposition of 1 Corinthians 12–14.* Grand Rapids: Baker, 1987.

Cayne, Bernard S., ed. *Encyclopedia Americana.* International edition. Danbury, CT: Grolier, 1986. S.v. "David Bushnell" by Joyce L. Myers.

The Challenge. Denver. 2 September 1886; 4 March 1889. From Willard Scrapbook.

Clouse, Bonnidell, and Robert G. Clouse, eds. *Women in Ministry: Four Views.* Downers Grove: InterVarsity, 1989.

Conzelmann, Hans. *1 Corinthians.* Edited by George W. MacRae. Translated by James W. Leitch. Philadelphia: Fortress, 1975.

"A Crisis in the W.C.T.U." *Chicago Tribune,* 19 September 1897. From Willard Scrapbook.

Cross, F. L., and E. A. Livingstone, eds. *The Oxford Dictionary of the Christian Church.* 2d ed. New York: Oxford University Press, 1983.

Dayton, Lucille Sider, and Donald W. Dayton. "Women in the Holiness Movement." Unpublished manuscript, 1974.

"Defer to Lady Henry." *Chicago Times-Herald,* 1 August 1897. From Willard Scrapbook.

"Displeased with Lady Henry." *Kansas City Star,* 8 January 1898. From Willard Scrapbook.

Dowd, Sharyn. "1 Corinthians 14:34–35 as a Corinthian Slogan: The Old Roots of a 'New' Interpretation." Unpublished paper read at the Southeastern Regional Meeting of the Society for Biblical Literature, 16 March 1990.

Evans, Mary J. *Woman in the Bible.* Downers Grove: InterVarsity, 1983.

Fee, Gordon D. *The First Epistle to the Corinthians.* New International Commentary on the New Testament. Grand Rapids: Eerdmans, 1987.

Fitzpatrick, Kathleen. *Lady Henry Somerset.* Boston: Little, Brown, and Company, 1923.

Foh, Susan T. *Women and the Word of God: A Response to Biblical Feminism.* Phillipsburg, NJ: Presbyterian and Reformed, 1979.

"A Good Work." Chicago. *The Inter Ocean,* 13 February 1886. From Willard Scrapbook.

Gray, K. Fillmore. "Crusader: California Woman's career reads like a movie scenario." *The Christian Advocate,* 8 January 1942. Photocopy received from Peg Moor, great-niece of Bushnell.

Gustafson, Zadel Barnes. "Frances E. Willard." *The Christian* 981 (2 December 1887). From Willard Scrapbook.

Halsey, William D., ed. *Collier's Encyclopedia.* New York: Macmillan Educational Company, 1985. S.v. "Horace Bushnell" by Barbara M. Cross.

Harper, Joyce. *Women and the Gospel.* Pinner, Great Britain: C.B.R.F. Publications, 1974.

Hay-Cooper, L. *Josephine Butler and Her Work for Social Purity.* London: Society for Promoting Christian Knowledge, 1922.

Hearn, Ginny. "New Publishers of Katharine Bushnell." *Update: Newsletter of the Evangelical Women's Caucus* 11 (winter 1987–88): 7–8.

Hoppin, Ruth. "The Legacy of Katharine Bushnell." *Update: Newsletter of the Evangelical Women's Caucus* 11 (winter 1987–88): 5–6.

Hull, Gretchen Gaebelein. *Equal to Serve: Women and Men in the Church and Home.* Old Tappan, NJ: Revell, 1987.

The Inter Ocean. Chicago. 13, 15 February 1886.

Jewett, Paul K. *Man as Male and Female.* Grand Rapids: Eerdmans, 1975.

Johnson, George W., and Lucy A. Johnson. *Josephine E. Butler: An Autobiographical Memoir.* 3d ed. Bristol, England: J. W. Arrowsmith, 1928.

Kaiser, W. C. "Paul, Women and the Church." *Worldwide Challenge* 3 (1976): 9–12.

Keir, J. Howard. "Neither Male nor Female: An Examination of the Status of Women in the New Testament." *Evangelical Quarterly* 55 (1983): 31–42.

Koenig, John. *Charismata: God's Gifts for God's People.* Philadelphia: Westminster, 1978.

"Lady Henry May Stay." *Chicago Times-Herald,* 30 July 1897. From Willard Scrapbook.

"Lady Henry Somerset Retracts." *Chicago Tribune,* 7 February 1898. From Willard Scrapbook.

"Lady Henry Somerset's Letter." *Chicago Post,* 8 February 1898. From Willard Scrapbook.

"Last Will and Testament of Katharine C. Bushnell." Photocopy sent from Bushnell's niece, Jean O'Rourk, to Ruth Hoppin.

Laws of Wisconsin. Chapter 214, Laws of 1887, no. 46, S. Photocopy received from The State of Wisconsin Legislative Reference Bureau, Madison, Wisconsin.

MacGorman, Jack W. *The Gifts of the Spirit: An Exposition of 1 Corinthians 12–14.* Nashville: Broadman, 1974.

Martin, Ralph P. *The Spirit and the Congregation: Studies in 1 Corinthians 12–15.* Grand Rapids: Eerdmans, 1984.

Maxwell, L. E. *Women in Ministry.* With a foreword by Ted S. Rendall, and introduction by Ruth C. Dearing. Wheaton: Victor, 1987.

McDowell, Mary E. "A Noble Defender." *The Union Signal* 15 (4 November 1889), 5 (WCTU microflim edition), roll 5, frame 425.

"Minutes of National Women's Christian Temperance Union Convention." 1884, xliv, xlv. Photocopy received from Frances Willard Memorial Library for Alcohol Research, National Women's Christian Temperance Union, Evanston, Illinois.

Montgomery, Helen Barrett. *Centenary Translation of the New Testament.* Philadelphia: American Baptist Publication Society, 1924.

————. "Good Books for Busy Pastors." *The Baptist* S (1924–25): 557–58.

Moorman, John R. H. *A History of the Church in England.* 3d ed. London: Adam & Charles Black, 1976.

Morris, Leon. *The First Epistle of Paul to the Corinthians.* Grand Rapids: Eerdmans, 1958.

The National Union Catalog Pre-1956 Imprints. Vol. 87. London: Mansell Information/Publishing Ltd., 1970.

Oakland Tribune, 10 February 1946. Photocopy of obituary sent by manager of Truman's Funeral Directors.

Odell-Scott, David W. "Let the Women Speak in Church: An Egalitarian Interpretation of 1 Cor 14:33b–36." *Biblical Theology Bulletin* 13 (1983): 90–93.

Orr, William F., and James Arthur Walther. *I Corinthians.* Vol. 32 of the Anchor Bible. Edited by William Foxwell Albright and David Noel Freedman. Garden City, NY: Doubleday, 1976.

Osborn, Henry J. "Close of the Anti-Opium Campaign in England. *The Union Signal* 21 (18 April 1895), 4 (WCTU microfilm edition), roll 10, frame 250.

"Our Third and Fourth Round-the-World Missionaries in the Orient." *The Union Signal* 16 (23 August 1894), 3–4 (WCTU microfilm edition), roll 9, frame 569.

"Our Third and Fourth Round-the-World Missionaries in the Orient." *The Union Signal* 20 (23 August 1894), 4 (WCTU microfilm edition), roll 9, frame 569.

"The Outcome of a Noble Work." *The Union Signal* 19 (5 October 1893), 9 (WCTU microfilm edition), roll 9, frame 171.

Penn-Lewis, Jessie. *The "Magna Charta" of Woman According to the Scriptures.* Bournemouth, England: The Overcomer Book Room, 1919; reprint, Minneapolis: Bethany Fellowship, 1975.

Petrie, Glen. *A Singular Iniquity: The Campaigns of Josephine Butler.* New York: Viking, 1971.

"Points from Lake Bluff Training School." *The Union Signal* 12 (26 August 1886), 2 (WCTU microfilm edition), roll 3, frame 376.

Poole, Mary A. Ward. "English Farewells." *The Union Signal* 19 (14 September 1893), 5 (WCTU microfilm edition), roll 9, frame 140.

"A Quick History of the C. D. Acts." *The Union Signal* 20 (21 June 1894), 9 (WCTU microfilm edition), roll 9, frame 512.

Rambau. *Commentary on the Torah: Genesis.* New York: Shilo, 1971.

Robinson, A. T., and Alfred Plummer. *A Critical and Exegetical Commentary on the First Epistle of St. Paul to the Corinthians.* New York: Charles Scribner's Sons, 1911.

Smith, Mrs. G. C. "Social Purity Work." *The Union Signal* 13 (5 May 1887), 12 (WCTU microfilm edition), roll 4, frame 149.

Starr, Lee Anna. *The Bible Status of Woman.* New York: New York Lithographing Corp., 1926; reprint, Zarephath, NJ: Pillar of Fire, 1955.

Stout, William Bushnell. *So Away I Went*. New York: Bobbs-Merrill, 1951.

"Sustain Dr. Kate Bushnell." *W.C.T.U. State Work* 4 (March 1889).

Talbert, C. H. "Paul's Understanding of the Holy Spirit: The Evidence of 1 Corinthians 12–14." In *Perspectives on the New Testament: Essays in Honor of Frank Stagg*, edited by C. H. Talbert, 95–108. Macon, GA: Mercer University Press, 1984.

Thomas, Griffith. Review of *God's Word to Women* by Katharine C. Bushnell, in *The Sunday School Times*, 22 March 1924.

Tischler, Nancy M. *Legacy of Eve: Women of the Bible*. Atlanta: John Knox, 1977.

Trible, Phyllis. *God and the Rhetoric of Sexuality*. Philadelphia: Fortress, 1978.

"Truth about the Fielding Case." *W.C.T.U. State Work* 4 (June 1889), 5.

W.C.T.U. State Work. Madison, Wisconsin. 2 (December 1887); 3 (November 1888); 4 (March 1889).

"Want Lady Somerset to Remain." *Boston Herald*, 30 July 1897, 1. From Willard Scrapbook.

Willard, Frances E. "Dr. Kate Bushnell, A Sketch." *The Union Signal* 16 (20 November 1890), 4 (WCTU microfilm edition), roll 6, frame 512.

———. *Glimpses of Fifty Years: The Autobiography of an American Woman*. Chicago: H. J. Smith & Co., 1889.

———. "Our White-Ribbon Anchorage." *The Union Signal* 18 (20 October 1892), 9 (WCTU microfilm edition), roll 8, frame 282.

———. *Woman in the Pulpit*. Boston: D. Lothrup Company, 1888.

Willard, Frances E., ed. *A Woman of the Century*. Buffalo, NY: Moolton, 1893.

Women's Medical School: Northwestern University (Woman's Medical College of Chicago) Class Histories 1870–1890. Chicago: H. G. Butler, Publisher, 1896.

The Union Signal. Chicago. 4 March, 22 April, 1 July, 26 August 1886; 11 January, 5 May 1887; 25 October, 8 November 1888; 10, 31 January, 21 February, 14 March, 11 April, 6 June, 4, 8 November, 26 December 1889; 20 November, 25 December 1890; 20 October, 8 December 1892; 4, 11 May, 15, 22 June, 9 August, 14, 21 September, 5 October, 2, 30 November, 18 December 1893; 29 March, 7, 14, 21 June, 5 July, 16, 23 August 1894; 26 March, 11 April, 1 August, 26 November, 17 December 1896; 1 July 1897. From National Headquarters, WCTU (Joint Ohio Historical Society—Michigan Historical Collections—WCTU microfilm edition).